First Published 2011
Reprinted and updated 2013
2QT Limited (Publishing),
Lancashire, UK
www.2qt.co.uk

Grateful thanks to Irene Newby for the photograph
of the sheep on the cover
Cover design by Greg Ashley
Typesetting by Peter Jackson

Printed in Slovenia on behalf of Latitude Press Limited.

A CIP catalogue record for this publication is available
from the British Library

ISBN 978-1-908098-37-5

MyWalkingGuide.com use Quo Digital Mapping (by Mapyx).
Mapping data in this guide (e.g. the Section profiles)
is reproduced with their kind permission.
www.mapyx.com

PLEASE NOTE

Whilst every effort has been made to make these notes as clear as possible, and care has been taken to ensure their accuracy, the written word can be open to misinterpretation.

In addition, the landscape itself can change–ranging from simple things such as gates replacing stiles, new signposts etc. to more major occurrences such as rivers being diverted and new roads being constructed.

The notes are intended to be used in conjunction with a map and compass and/or GPS, not as a substitute for them.

It is the responsibility of each walker to determine his or her level of fitness and navigational skill and please remember that there is no substitute for good, old-fashioned common sense.

Neither the author nor MyWalkingGuide.com can accept responsibility or liability for any accident or injury sustained on the walk.

THE CUMBRIA WAY
(from ULVERSTON to CARLISLE)
CONTENTS

ACKNOWLEDGEMENTS
Grateful thanks to all those authors whose books have provided information about hill-walking, Cumbria and the Cumbria Way. Special thanks to the Ramblers and Natural England whose websites have been used for much of the information in the pages on Access and Farm Animals and Wildlife.

WHAT'S INCLUDED IN THIS GUIDE BOOK?

This book is intended to be a practical guide for you to carry with you on the trail. It concentrates on the stuff you need to get from one place to the next, but also includes information that might come in handy–especially for those minor mishaps (such as bad weather) or in the unlikely event of anything going seriously wrong.

So, in order to keep the book to a manageable size certain things have had to be left out. This means, for example, that there is very little background information in here about the towns and villages that the Way passes through.

We have also had to sacrifice a lot of detail about planning the walk but, for purchasers of this book, this is all available as a free download from our website (www.mywalkingguide.com).

INFORMATION AVAILABLE FROM THE DOWNLOAD

Basically, everything to do with planning your holiday, including:

- Preparing for the walk–fitness and navigation skills
- Hints and tips on finding accommodation
- Some suggested itineraries
- Events taking place on or near the route of the CW
- A kit list
- Baggage transfer providers
- Getting to and from the CW
- An accommodation listing.

Plus

- Safety on the hills and first aid.

And a gazetteer of all the places of interest passed through on the route– a bit of history, things to see and do and all that gubbins.

WHAT TO DO IN AN EMERGENCY

The emergency telephone number in the UK is 999.
Whatever mishap might occur, the first thing is not to panic!

Reproduced below is the advice given by a Lake District mountain rescue team (MRT):

When to use a mobile phone to contact an MRT:

- If you or a member of your party sustains an injury warranting the assistance of an MRT;
- If you come across someone who has sustained an injury warranting the assistance of an MRT;
- If one of your party has become separated from the main party and you have made every effort to, but have been unable to meet up again;
- If you want to report having seen or heard any internationally recognised distress calls (usually six short blasts on a whistle, repeated at one-minute intervals. Sometimes flashes with a torch are used instead. The standard signal for replying is three short blasts/flashes, repeated at one-minute intervals).

When NOT to use a mobile phone to contact an MRT:

- Do not use the mobile phone at the "first sign of trouble": be self reliant if possible;
- Do not rely solely on the mobile phone as a safety device, there are areas of poor or no reception;
- The mobile phone is not a substitute for experience.

How to use:

- First make a note of all the relevant details (location, giving grid ref if possible; name, sex and age of casualty; nature of injuries or disability; number of people in party and intended destination; the number of the mobile phone in use);
- Ring 999 and ask for the Police (Cumbria Police for the CW);
- Explain what the call is about, giving the details as above;
- Do NOT change your position until contacted by the MRT, who will agree future protocol for use of phone.

IN CASE OF BAD WEATHER...

Make sure you get a weather forecast every morning before setting out. Cumbria is well served by the Lake District Weatherline–a Met Office weather service especially for walkers, climbers, cyclists etc. and available online at www.lakedistrictweatherline.co.uk or by phone on 0844 846 2444.

Usually, heavy rain is not dangerous in itself, but do be aware that mountain streams can fill with water very quickly to flood or become impossible to cross. Most of the main streams on the CW are crossed by footbridges so *should* be OK. The advice is that if you have to cross a swollen stream and there is no bridge, do NOT attempt to wade across–walk to the nearest bridge if you can, or walk upstream to find a safer crossing place...or turn back.

Thunderstorms are a different kettle of fish. Fortunately not all that common in the Lake District, lightning is not good news if you're out in the open, especially on high, exposed ridges. There are no narrow ridges on the CW but there is plenty of open ground. The best advice seems to be to find a low spot away from poles, trees and fences. You do not want to be the highest object around! If you think that the lightning is close, crouch down, balance on the balls of your feet, and put your hands on your knees with your head between them. This makes you a smaller target and minimises your contact with the ground. Do NOT seek shelter from the rain under boulders or under trees, as these may attract lightning themselves. Some people suggest moving walking poles etc. away to one side.

Strong winds can be dangerous, especially on exposed high ground and on ridges. The likeliest place on the CW for strong winds to be a problem is probably the section between Lingy Hut and Potts Gill (i.e. the High Pike summit area).

If you heed our advice about when to walk the CW, snow and ice are less likely to be a problem. If you do choose to walk in winter, do take care of icy rocks, especially when you're walking downhill.

Just to put things in perspective–in over 30 years of walking in the Lakes, the author has never had an emergency to deal with–apart from once leaving his packed lunch at home. Never again!

THE CUMBRIA WAY: AN OVERVIEW

The Cumbria Way (CW) is a multi-day walk (or trek) of just over 70 miles. It lies wholly within the county of Cumbria in north-west England. Nearly always walked from south to north, the CW starts in the market town of Ulverston on Morecambe Bay and runs through some of Britain's most scenic countryside to Cumbria's only city, Carlisle, almost at the border with Scotland.

The CW was developed by local branches of the Ramblers' Association after the county of Cumbria came into existence following local government reorganisation in 1974. Cumbria is made up of the old counties of Cumberland and Westmorland, plus the Furness part of Lancashire (Lancashire over the Sands, as it used to be known) and a small part of West Yorkshire. It contains England's largest National Park–the Lake District–as well as a good part of the Yorkshire Dales National Park, and is England's second-largest county.

Cumbria boasts a huge variety of scenery and the CW has been carefully designed to pass through as many different types of landscape as possible given its fairly modest length. The scenic delights of the Lake District are generally well known but it is worth remembering that the CW is not just a Lake District walk–almost 30% of it lies outside the National Park boundary, and it is these non-Lake District sections that add to the charm and variety of the route.

Starting from Ulverston, the CW takes the walker through and over low rolling hills to reach the National Park boundary after just five miles. Gradually farmland gives way to wilder country, rocks are more in evidence, the terrain gets hillier and there is an early glimpse of Coniston Water. By the time lonely Beacon Tarn is reached, nearly 10 miles into the walk, some of the bigger hills (fells) of the Lake District look almost close enough to reach out and touch.

One of the joys of the CW is how the first stage of the journey familiarises the walker with the high fells. Before nearly everybody started coming to the Lakes by car, the classic way of getting to know the place was on foot from the most conveniently placed railway station so, in a sense, the CW is re-introducing us to a gentler and altogether more satisfying way of travelling.

After a glorious three-mile walk along the shore of Coniston Water, the CW takes us to the village of Coniston, once a busy mining and quarrying centre but now given over almost entirely to tourism. For the next 30 miles or so, the CW leads through some of the most spectacular–and best-known–landscapes that the UK has to offer. In order, the CW visits: the lake and wooded shores of Tarn Hows, the waterfalls of Colwith Force and Skelwith Force, the delightful lake (and village) of Elterwater, the hugely impressive rocky skyline at the head of Great Langdale (including the evocatively named Dungeon Ghyll), the wild country at the top of Stake Pass, lonely Langstrath, fabulous wooded Borrowdale, and the shores of Derwentwater–from where there are several opportunities to take a trip on the launch to Keswick.

The small town of Keswick lies just over half way along the CW and, with its wide choice of shops and accommodation, makes an ideal staging post. Many walkers arrange to have a short day into Keswick to allow them the opportunity for a rest or a little exploration. Beyond Keswick the Way climbs into the hills for an exhilarating walk to remote Skiddaw House and then on into the empty country of Skiddaw Forest. A modest climb over High Pike (at 2157 ft the CW's only summit) is followed by an easy descent through the abandoned mine-workings of Potts Gill and so to the pretty village of Caldbeck.

Most of the final stage of the Way is a walk along the banks of the River Caldew and the speed of the transition from the wild country of Skiddaw Forest to the gentle farmland of the valley is almost startling. The CW's approach to the city of Carlisle remains peaceful and rural for all but the last couple of miles, and the route finds a way to visit one of Carlisle's gems, its Cathedral, before finishing at the Market Cross in the city centre.

Although the grandeur and the variety of the landscapes on the CW are outstanding, there is much more to the walk than just the scenery. The towns and villages themselves are interesting with much to explore, and there is a rich industrial heritage to discover–mining, quarrying, water mills, a pencil factory, even a gunpowder works - almost all of them disused now but traces remain for all to see, even though some have been converted into housing or holiday accommodation.

And, when you're not out actually doing the walk, you can learn about the colourful parade of eminent personalities who had strong connections with places on the route–from comic actor Stan Laurel (who was born in Ulverston) to speed ace Donald Campbell, who died on Coniston Water in his attempt to break his own world water speed record; and from the great polymath, John Ruskin, whose grave is in Coniston churchyard to the huntsman John Peel who is buried at Caldbeck.

Just one or two points about the route:

- Transport links to and from both ends of the route are good;
- Public transport on the route ranges from OK to non-existent;
- Accommodation is plentiful in some places (e.g. Keswick) and very sparse in others (e.g. for most of the way between Keswick and Carlisle);
- Waymarking and signposting exists but there are gaps–that's one of the reasons that this guide will be useful!

As long-distance walks go, the CW is not generally regarded as being all that tough: its modest length means it can be comfortably walked by most reasonably fit walkers in under a week and, for the most part, the route threads a way through the hills, rather than over them. But, most of the walk is not flat: there are lots of ups and downs and the miles have to be earned. If done in one go, as a single journey, then, as with any multi-day trek, its completion ranks as a considerable achievement. And don't let anybody tell you different!

WHEN TO WALK THE CUMBRIA WAY

It is theoretically possible to walk the CW at any time of year. However, the weather tends to be colder, wetter and windier in the winter months and the daylight hours are much shorter–on a wet day in December it can quite easily be going dark by 3 p.m. In addition, many of the facilities on the route–accommodation, refreshment and public transport–are not as readily available in the winter.

For all these reasons, we strongly recommend that you walk the CW between April and October. If you want the solitude and the challenges that winter walking can bring, prepare accordingly and don't say we didn't warn you!

POINTS TO BE AWARE OF.
POTENTIAL DIFFICULTIES ON THE CUMBRIA WAY

The CW is not a wilderness route, being generally not very far from roads, broad tracks or habitations. But there are places where, by English standards, the walker may feel remote, being some hours from the nearest place of refuge or refreshment.

Not all roads carry a bus route, and those bus routes that do exist may not run all year or on every day of the week. Public transport provision in rural England is not as comprehensive as it is in the cities. So, if you think you may need to make use of bus or train (or launch) services while on the trail, **please make sure you have a look at the timetables in advance**. Some information (**but not the timetables**) is given on the page about Public Transport.

Escape routes are mentioned in the route notes, and facilities available (e.g. refreshments, telephone boxes and public transport) are shown at the start of each Section.

And don't forget: the route notes are intended to be used with a map and compass (and GPS if you have one).

Ulverston to Coniston (or Torver):

Easy walking but quite a long way with lots of little ups and downs, and no refreshments available en route. Some buses available but diversion off the route to the nearest bus-stop may be necessary.

Coniston to Skelwith Bridge:

No public transport, telephones or refreshments etc.

Skelwith Bridge to Dungeon Ghyll:

No special problems.

Dungeon Ghyll to Rosthwaite:

A stiff climb to Stake Pass although the path is good and should not pose serious navigation problems. Remember that Langstrath is a long valley with no shelter.

Rosthwaite to Keswick:

No special problems.

Keswick to Caldbeck:

A long way without shelter, whichever of the two alternative routes is chosen. Skiddaw House youth hostel is not open during the day. Apart from turning back to Keswick, the only places where you might find refuge are Mosedale (seasonal tea room, a couple of B&Bs and an infrequent bus service) and Bassenthwaite (pub, B&Bs and a bus service).

If caught in very poor weather at Skiddaw House, the easiest line is to follow the land-rover track to Peter House, or you could turn around and return to Keswick where buses and/or taxis might make a better option. Parts of the section between Carrock Mine and Potts Gill on the main route are without clear paths.

NB There are old mine workings at Carrock Mine and Potts Gill. The author is not aware of any unfenced shafts near the route but that isn't to say they don't exist. **Take great care near any old mine workings.**

Caldbeck to Carlisle:

One or two tricky bits early on (but you have these notes!): thereafter any problems are more to do with distance and, until Bridge End is reached, lack of facilities.

A note about telephones on the CW

Mobile phone signals are poor or even non-existent on certain parts of the Cumbria Way, notably in the parts furthest from the towns and villages, as well as in steep-sided valleys. This applies to much of the route so it would not be wise to rely on being able to use your mobile. Public call boxes are not all that common either and the ones in the most remote areas are mentioned in the route notes. They do not all accept coins. You can use a debit or credit card (instructions in the phone box), or you can buy a phone card (available in multiples of £5) from a Post Office. The instructions are on the reverse of the card with a scratch-off PIN.

PUBLIC TRANSPORT ON THE CUMBRIA WAY

This is not an exhaustive list, merely a summary of where to find details about those services that might be useful:

Train

To Ulverston and from Carlisle to get to and from CW
From Dalston to Carlisle on the route
www.nationalrail.co.uk

Bus

To Ulverston and from Carlisle to get to and from CW
www.gouk.about.com or www.nationalexpress.com

For buses on the route www.travelline.info (0871 200 22 33)
or www.cumbria.gov.uk

Route	Service
Ulverston - Torver - Coniston	X12
Coniston - Ambleside	505
Ambleside - Skelwith Br - Dungeon Ghyll	516
Ambleside - Keswick	555
Borrowdale - Keswick	77 and 78
Keswick - Mosedale - Caldbeck	73
Bassenthwaite - Keswick	X58
Caldbeck - Bridge End - Dalston - Carlisle	74
Bridge End - Carlisle	65, 74 and 75
Dalston - Carlisle	74 and 75

Launches

Coniston	www.conistonlaunch.co.uk	017687 75753
Derwentwater	www.keswick-launch.co.uk	017687 72263

TOURIST INFORMATION CENTRES ON OR NEAR THE CW

Ulverston	01229 587120
Coniston	015394 41533
Ambleside (for Langdale)	015394 32729
Keswick	017687 72645
Carlisle	01228 625600

Opening times vary but typically are from 9.30am until 5pm.

TAXI SERVICES ON THE CUMBRIA WAY

Please note: most of this information has been obtained from the Internet and **no recommendation is given or implied.**

Ulverston	D & B Taxis	01229 586038;
	Geoff's Taxis	01229 586666;
	IC Taxis	**01229 582765;**
	Paul's Taxis	01229 586669;
	A2B	01229 587030;
	McKenna's	01229 582180
Coniston	Sarah's Taxis	015394 41171
Ambleside (for Langdale)		
	Ambleside Taxis	015394 33842;
	Kevin's Taxis	015394 32371;
	John's Taxis	015394 32857
Keswick (also for Borrowdale)		
	Davies Taxis	**017687 72676**;
	Derwent Taxis	017687 75585;
	DNK	017687 74959;
	Keswick Cab Co (Keswick Taxis)	**0800 633 5746**
Caldbeck	Try Keswick Cab Co (0800 633 5746) or there are two companies based in Wigton:	
	Thomason Travel	016973 44116
	Station House Taxis	016973 43148
Carlisle	Beeline Taxis	01228 534440;
	Metro Taxis	01228 522088;
	Radio Cabs	01228 527575;
	City Cabs	01228 520000

Those **shown in bold** offer a baggage transfer service.

MAPS NEEDED FOR THE CUMBRIA WAY

We recommend the Ordnance Survey (OS) Outdoor Leisure (OL) maps which, at a scale of 1:25,000 (about 2½ inches to the mile), are perfect for navigating by. (The 1:50,000 Landranger series are also OK but they do not show field boundaries.)

For the CW, you need all four of the OS Lake District OL maps:

- OL6 South-western area (for Ulverston to Coniston, and Oak Howe (Great Langdale) to Stake Pass);
- OL7 South-eastern area (for Coniston to Oak Howe);
- OL4 North-western area (for Stake Pass to Keswick and then on to Skiddaw House and Fell Side);
- OL5 North-eastern area (for Fell Side (or Skiddaw House) to Caldbeck and on to Buckabank near Dalston).

For the last 4 or 5 miles to Carlisle you also need Explorer map 315 Carlisle.

A less expensive–and possibly more convenient–option is to use the Harvey Cumbria Way map. At 1:40,000 it lacks some of the detail shown on the OL maps but the whole route is on one map, and is easy on the eye. Excellent for planning purposes!

WEATHER ON THE CUMBRIA WAY

Weather in the north-west of England is notoriously fickle: it can do just about anything at any time of year! In general, the period from April to October gives better (warmer and drier) weather than the winter months, but there are no guarantees.

Harsh winters had become almost a thing of the past but recent years have seen a return to snow and ice. For most walkers the main problems are wind and rain, the two very often coming together, and nearly always with low cloud and therefore poor visibility. Not only does this make the walking itself more demanding, but you may also have to be prepared for mud in the lowland areas and even flooded footpaths (e.g. on the stretch leading to Elterwater village).

Having the right clothing to keep you warm and dry is a must– see the Kit List (download) for more information.

A NOTE ON ACCOMMODATION ON THE CUMBRIA WAY

Whether you're camping or staying in the swankiest of hotels, it is always safer to book your accommodation in advance, and the vast majority of you will probably have done that. Parts of the route get very busy, especially at weekends and in summer, so those not booking ahead might experience difficulties.

Some guidebooks to the Lakes and the CW emphasise how abundant accommodation in Cumbria is. Well, yes, it is...but it's not always where you want it (there's very little between Ulverston and Torver for example, or between Keswick and Caldbeck, or between Caldbeck and Carlisle). And, however much there might be, it's not a lot of use to you if it's full when you arrive.

The "Facilities" pages in each Section list all the settlements where accommodation may be available, and purchasers of this book can also download our Accommodation Listing at no extra cost.

Tourist Information Centres (TICs) on the route may also be able to help, and do not rule out the possibility of using public transport (or taxi) to ferry you back and forth to accommodation if things get tight.

Particular problems to be aware of include:

- **Ulverston** hosts two Buddhist Festivals each year. There is a Buddhist Meditation Centre at Conishead Priory on the edge of the town, and the week-long spring festival and the two-week summer festival attract followers from all over the world. This, unsurprisingly, means that accommodation in the town is hard to come by during those times. In 2011 the dates were 25 May to 1 June and 22 July to 6 August. Have a look at www.ulverston.co.uk for details. Some B&Bs in Coniston offer lifts to Ulverston (or there is a handily-timed bus service), or you could consider staying your first night in somewhere like Grange-over-Sands and taking a train to the start of the CW.
- Similiarly, **Keswick** is home to a three-week Christian Convention in July/August every year. It attracts large numbers of people as does the Jazz Festival in May. Details at www.keswick.org .

WALKING IN ENGLAND –
A NOTE ON ACCESS AND RIGHTS OF WAY

For people new to the joys of walking in England, please be aware that you can't just walk where the fancy takes you. Most of the land in England (and Wales) is privately owned and access to it for members of the public is strictly controlled through a pretty complex set of laws.

However, in practice, especially on a trail as well-walked as the Cumbria Way, there should be no access problems at all. England and Wales are blessed with a fantastic network of "public rights of way": these include footpaths, bridleways and by-ways and walkers have legal access to all of these. England alone has about 118,000 miles (190,000 km) of public rights of way (PRoWs), and many of these are waymarked and/or signposted in some way. They are also shown on the 1:25,000 and 1:50,000 Ordnance Survey Maps, and on the Harvey maps.

In addition to PRoWs, there are "Permissive (or Permitted or Concessionary) Footpaths". These don't have the same legal status as PRoW's but are paths whose use by the public is allowed by the landowner.

Of great interest to hill-walkers in particular is "access land". Under the Countryside and Rights of Way (CRoW) Act, introduced in 2004, the public can now walk freely on mapped areas of "mountain, moor, heath and downland" without having to stick to paths and PRoWs. In some cases (e.g. in the upland parts of the Lake District) walkers have always had this "freedom to roam", but seeing it enshrined as the law of the land was a major victory for access groups such as the Ramblers. Access Land is clearly marked on OS maps in a pale brown colour, and there is often a sign affixed to gates etc. as you enter and leave access land. To find out more about access and rights of way, have a look at this website: www.naturalengland.org.uk .

So far as the CW is concerned, anybody sticking to the official route or any of the diversions described in these route notes should have no difficulties with access at all. If you are challenged, the chances are you are not on the CW, so please do as the farmer/landowner etc. asks. **If you do have any difficulties please let us know, giving as much detail as possible.**

FARM ANIMALS AND WILDLIFE

Some walkers–especially visitors to the UK–are surprised at how much of the route they have to share with farm animals. This is usually sheep, but can also mean cattle (cows **and** bulls) and horses, not to mention dogs and various types of poultry in farm yards. The simplest advice to give and to follow is to ignore farm animals and the chances are that they will ignore you. Animals on the route of the CW will probably be used to seeing walkers troop past, and should not be bothered by your presence.

However, one golden rule is to **never get between a cow and her calf**: cows are big animals and, when they think their young are threatened, can become aggressive. Regrettably, there have been serious injuries and even deaths where cows have trampled people. Having a dog with you makes matters worse. If you are threatened by cattle and you have a dog with you, let the dog off its lead–the dog will probably run away, and the cattle are less likely to bother you. There are quite complicated laws about keeping bulls in fields to which the public have legal access but, suffice it to say here, any bulls you come across should be with cows and should not pose any threat. Having said that, untethered bulls on their own and loose dogs should be treated with caution. The author is not aware of any serious incidents involving cows, bulls or dogs on the CW.

There are no wild animals to cause any great concern, although birds of prey such as buzzards can become very agitated if they think you're getting too near their nesting sites, particularly in June/July when their young are beginning to fly. A buzzard has sharp (and mucky) talons and if it draws blood, medical advice should be sought. There is, unfortunately, such a bird on the route of the CW–at Orthwaite on the western alternative to the main route between Keswick and Caldbeck. See the Section 4 route notes for the gruesome X-rated details.

The adder is the UK's only poisonous snake and, although it does occur in the Lake District, it is not common and the author is not aware that any parts of the CW are known habitats. They are, in any case, shy creatures who do their best to stay away from humans.

Ticks are a different matter and are a growing problem. Have a look at www.ramblers.org.uk/info/practical/safety.

WHAT DOES THAT MEAN?
(Sunday title "Glossary of Terms")

Guide books and other literature about walks and walking tend to be peppered with all manner of strange words, so we thought we'd cover a few of the commonest words that might cause doubt.

Beck–stream.

Cairn–a pile of stones, usually marking the path, a summit or a viewpoint. Some cairns are just heaps of stones while others are the work of craftsmen and are well-known landmarks.

Col–a gap between two hills. There is a nice little col just before Beacon Tarn on the first Section of the CW.

Force–waterfall.

Gill–stream, usually–but not always– in a steep-sided ravine (to distinguish it from "beck").

Kissing gate–a type of gate which can be pushed to give access to a small enclosure, then moved in the opposite direction to allow the walker through to the other side. The idea is to let walkers through but not livestock. They are sometimes a very tight squeeze, especially for walkers with large rucksacks. The official explanation for why they are so called is that the gate just "kisses" (or touches) the enclosure without having to be latched in any way. It is, though, more fun to believe the folklore that says that, once you're through the gate, you hold the gate closed until the next person offers you a kiss. All well and good, but it clearly depends on who your companions are and is pretty much a waste of time if you are on your own. Solo walkers hanging around waiting for someone to turn up are not likely to endear themselves to anyone.

Pitched path–a path made or repaired, using large stones.

Scree or **screes**–Loose rocks or stones which have been caused by erosion (by ice or water) of cliffs above.

Sheepfold–an enclosure for sheep. In Cumbria, they are stone-built and are usually circular or rectangular, and most are now disused.

Stile–a means of crossing a wall or fence and they come in many forms. Most commonly, they consist of a wooden step. You will also find:

> **squeeze stiles**–gaps in walls wide enough for most humans to squeeze through, but not livestock;
> **ladder stiles**–basically ladders on either side of a wall;
> **through stiles** (may also be called stone step stiles)–large flat stones in a wall which form a sort of stairway over the wall. So-called because the stones go through the wall;
>
> Various combinations of any of the above, sometimes involving gates.

Tarn–a small mountain lake or pool.

Trig point–abbreviation for trigonometrical station or triangulation pillar. A plinth of concrete or stone, usually on a summit. They were once used for taking trigonometrical readings to determine the accurate location of surrounding features. Although their original function has been taken over by aerial photography and digital mapping, trig points remain helpful landmarks and navigational aids for hill-walkers.

THE COUNTRYSIDE CODE

The Countryside Code, reproduced below, is an updated version of the former Country Code, which was introduced in the 1950s. The update was considered timely after the introduction of the Countryside and Rights of Way Act (CRoW Act) in 2004.

As you can see, the Code is not difficult, and it is hoped that all walkers will keep to its simple and sensible requests. To see the Code in more detail, and any other related matters, please see www.naturalengland.gov.uk .

- Be safe, plan ahead and follow any signs
- Leave gates and property as you find them
- Protect plants and animals and take your litter home
- Keep dogs under close control
- Consider other people.

THE ROUTE NOTES–HOW TO USE

The main aim of these route notes is to enable you to walk the Cumbria Way without the worry and hassle that route-finding sometimes causes. They are, so far as we are aware, the most detailed and comprehensive route notes available and they are designed to be as clear and user-friendly as possible. It would be foolish of us to *guarantee* that you won't get lost, but the intention is to provide notes that are clear and unambiguous, and we have paid particular attention to those places which are known to have caused confusion and difficulty for walkers in the past.

Having said that, the notes are intended to be used **in conjunction with a map and compass, not as a substitute for them**. The written word can be interpreted by the reader to mean something different from what the author intended so, if there are doubts at any point, the map should be consulted for clarification. The use of frequent waypoints (see next paragraph) means also that, even if you do go astray, navigating to the next waypoint will put you back on track.

The route notes are split into numbered paragraphs, each taking the walker from one "waypoint" (WP) to the next. The WPs are intended to make navigation easier: they are either significant places in themselves (e.g. junctions of tracks) or are identifiable points that can be navigated to so as to take the walker across potentially confusing ground. GPS users will, of course, be familiar with the routine of navigating by WPs, but it is hoped that they will be found useful for other walkers too.

We have identified 136 WPs on the Cumbria Way and there are photos in the notes of (or from) those places where we know difficulties with route-finding exist. There are other photos scattered through the text to help with identification and to act as a reassurance that you're on the right track! The photos are not especially designed to look pretty but to illustrate what you should be seeing in front of you: if some of them look pretty as well, then that's a bonus!

The CW has some stretches of wild, open country to cross but, from a navigational point of view, much of the doubt on the route will be at lower levels where farmland has to be negotiated.

We think that most walkers will agree that navigating through farmland can be far more awkward and time-consuming than walking on high, open ground. Admittedly, going astray in a valley is not likely to be a matter of life and death, but it can cause a great deal of frustration to the walker and to the land owner or tenant who has to make his or her living there.

Places on the route that are known to have caused navigational problems include:

- several junctions and farmland footpaths on the Way between Ulverston and Beacon Tarn, (for example approaching Stony Crag Farm, leaving Broughton Beck and the fields near Kendall Ground);
- Stable Harvey Moss between Beacon Tarn and Coniston Water;
- the long section over High Pike from Carrock Mine to Nether Row on the main (eastern) route from Skiddaw House to Caldbeck;
- the section between Peter House and Orthwaite on the western (lower-level) option between Skiddaw House and Caldbeck;
- one or two spots between Caldbeck and Sebergham Bridge.

For the purposes of this guide, the route has been divided into five Sections of roughly equal length, and the detailed notes for each Section are preceded by a short introduction and a Section profile, which shows the ups and downs you'll have to negotiate. Don't worry, the vertical scale is greatly exaggerated. There is also a sketch map of each Section to enable you to see how everything "fits together", and the "Facilities" pages for each Section give information on such things as public transport, refreshments, accommodation and emergency escapes.

Please note that these Sections are not intended to represent recommended daily stages for the walk. Suggested itineraries are provided with the downloadable Information Pack that comes free of charge to buyers of this book.

Regarding the notes themselves, distances are given in metres and kilometres and heights in metres (to make it easier to use the notes in conjunction with the map). We have not included any map extracts with the notes on the grounds that all walkers using these notes will (or should) have a map with them already.

We haven't, as a general rule, given estimated times from WP to WP, mainly because people walk at different speeds, and because people do stop from time to time! When we say, "a few minutes", that just means a short time–less than 15 minutes, say. If you estimate a walking speed of something between 3 and 4 km per hour, you won't be far wrong–and most walkers are slower on the uphill bits than on the flat!

We'd be grateful if you would please let us know of any inaccuracies in these notes and, just as important, please let us have any suggestions for changes or improvements.

For those who are interested, the WP co-ordinates are given in the text as 12-digit Ordnance Survey grid references, split into two blocks of six–eastings and northings. To convert this into a standard 6-digit grid reference, simply knock off the first and the last two digits of each six-digit block and you have a six-digit grid reference which you can then locate in the usual way, and these are also shown. For example E 332329 N 502846 (WP 049 at High Park Farm) becomes 323 028.

The approximate distance to the next WP is given immediately below the paragraph number in the notes. Most of the waypoint co-ordinates were obtained on-site from a GPS receiver, but some were found later from digital mapping software. You may well find that many of the WP co-ordinates will not be exactly at the junction, gate or stile etc. that they refer to. Some of the co-ordinates were entered from where photographs were taken for example. But they will all be close enough for all practical purposes. ***If this is not the case, please let us know!*** *And if this is all gobbledygook to you, don't worry. You can still enjoy walking the Cumbria Way without bothering with the technicalities of grid references and all that malarkey.*

ABBREVIATIONS USED IN THE ROUTE NOTES

ATM	Automated teller machine (cash point/ hole in the wall etc.)	NW	North-west
		OS	Ordnance Survey
BW	Bridleway	R	Right
CW	Cumbria Way	RH	Right Hand
E	East	RoW	Right of Way
ENE	East-north-east	S	South
ESE	East-south-east	SE	South-east
FB	Footbridge	SP	Signpost
FP	Footpath	SSE	South-south-east
KG	Kissing gate	SSW	South-south-west
km	Kilometre(s)	STS	Stone through stile
L	Left	SW	South-west
LDNPA	Lake District National Park Authority	TIC	Tourist Information Centre
LH	Left Hand	W	West
LS	Ladder stile	WM	Waymark
m	Metres	WM'd	Waymarked
mins	Minutes	WMA	Waymark arrow
N	North	WMP	Waymark post
NE	North-east	WNW	West-north-west
NNE	North-north-east	WP	Waypoint
NNW	North-north-west	WSW	West-south-west
NP	National Park	YH(A)	Youth Hostel

A NOTE ABOUT THE SKETCH MAPS

Sketch maps are given at the beginning of the route notes for each Section of the route. They are there simply to show where the route goes in relation to such features as the nearest roads with a bus service and the hills that you are likely to be walking near. **They are most definitely NOT intended as navigational aids**.

They are based on Out of Copyright 1 inch to 1 mile OS Maps but the scale in this book is a little less than that.

NB The red roads on the maps are those with a (useful) bus service.

GETTING TO THE START OF THE CUMBRIA WAY

The start of the CW is at The Gill, a car-parking area on the west side of Ulverston town centre.

From the railway station walk up Springfield Rd and cross the main A590 road at the traffic lights. Continue ahead onto Queen St, which soon becomes King St. Less than 100m along King St, turn left on to Upper Brook St. At the end of this narrow street, you reach the Gill, an area of old cottages, small shops and a large car park. The walk begins at the far side of the car park, where the modern conical structure of steel and stone makes an impressive official starting point.

Ulverston town centre was not designed with the motor car in mind. If some kind soul is giving you a lift to the start of the walk, we suggest you find whatever public car parking you see a signpost to, and walk to The Gill from there.

ULVERSTON TOWN CENTRE

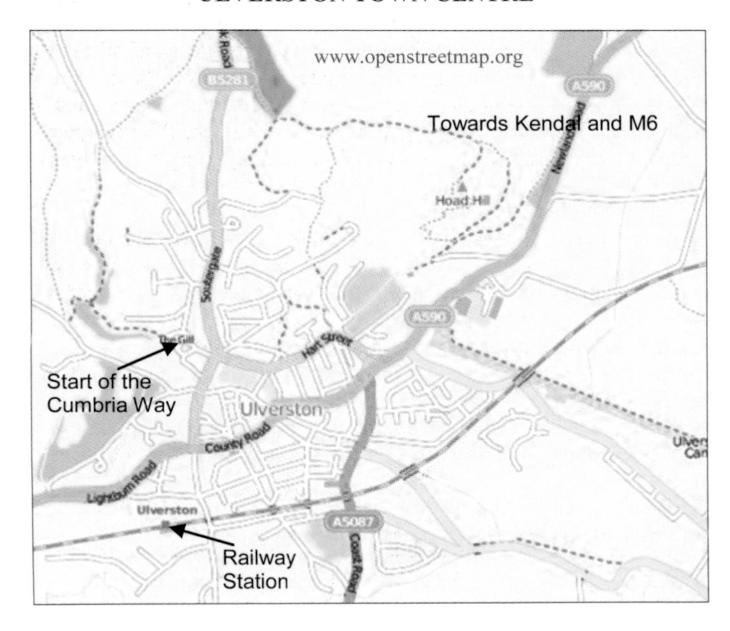

SECTION 1: ULVERSTON TO CONISTON

25.2km (15¾ miles); 650m (2100 ft) of ascent (approx).

If walked in one day in its entirety, this Section from Ulverston to Coniston can be a tough proposition, especially for the start of a multi-day trek. Some people skip it altogether and start the CW at Coniston, but they are depriving themselves of a grand walk that includes one of the best views on the entire journey (from Beacon Tarn) and one of its most typical Lakeland strolls (along the shore of Coniston Water). If you think nearly 16 miles and over 2,000 ft of ascent is too much, then you might be better off finishing at Torver on the first day and adjusting your itinerary accordingly. The diversion to Torver is described in these notes and it reduces the distance covered on the first day by nearly 5km (3 miles).

As you can see from the Profile, there are lots of ups and downs, and there can be plenty of mud and muck, especially along the early part of the route and after rain. Waymarking is pretty good on the whole, but there are places where you will be glad of these notes to help remove any doubts. The first half of the Section, from Ulverston to Kiln Bank, is through rolling farmland with lots of gates and stiles to slow you down. Thereafter, the landscape becomes a little more rugged and the walking more open. Arrival at Beacon Tarn is a real highlight and, if you do the whole Section in one go, the final part alongside Coniston Water is easy (but possibly longer than you would like).

There are no shops (and no cafés or pubs etc.) on the line of today's route so you will have to leave Ulverston with enough supplies of food, drink, emergency stuff and optimism to see you through the day. Public transport is not great either and there are very few phone boxes. To all intents and purposes, you're on your own!

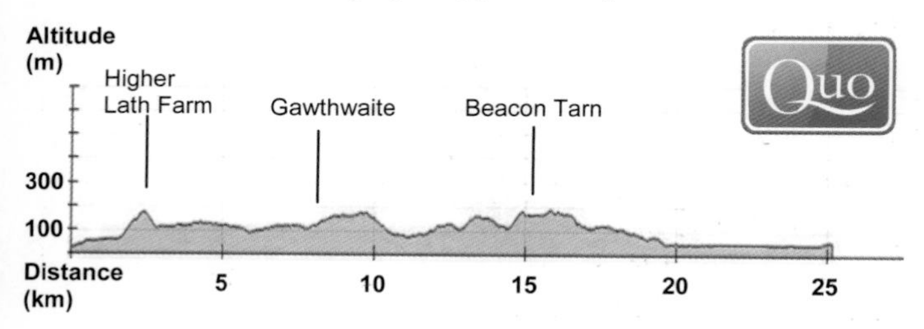

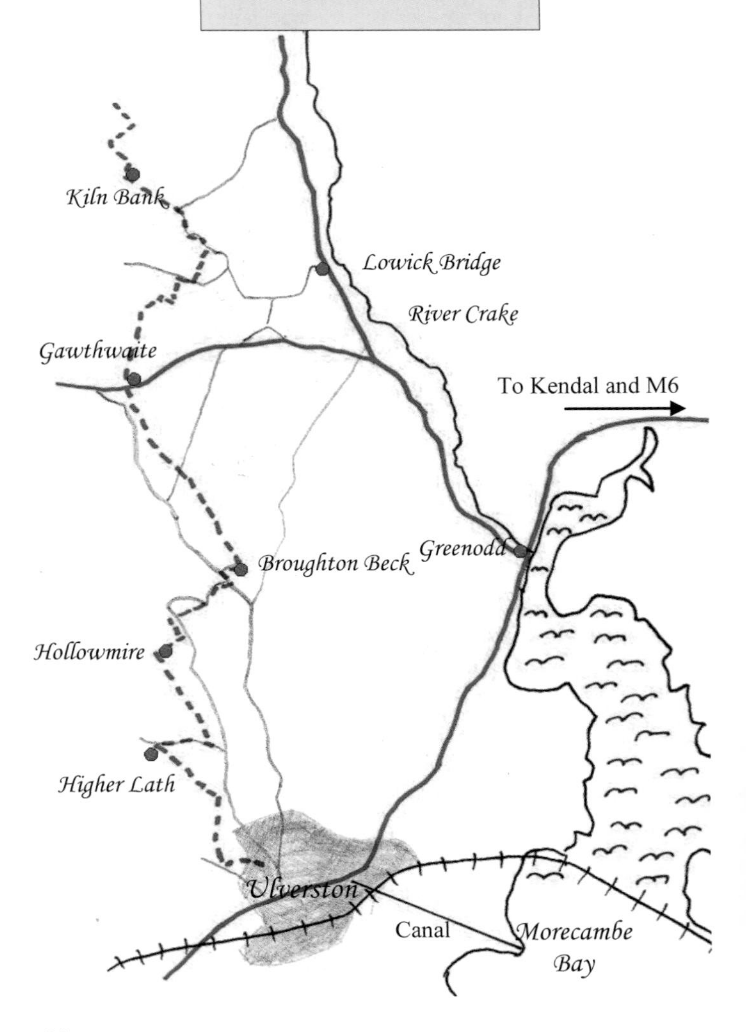
CUMBRIA WAY
SECTION 1 (South)
Ulverston to Kiln Bank
12km (7¾miles)
Kiln Bank
Lowick Bridge
River Crake
Gawthwaite
To Kendal and M6
Greenodd
Broughton Beck
Hollowmire
Higher Lath
Ulverston
Canal
Morecambe
Bay

CUMBRIA WAY
SECTION 1 (North)
Kiln Bank to Coniston
13km (8miles)

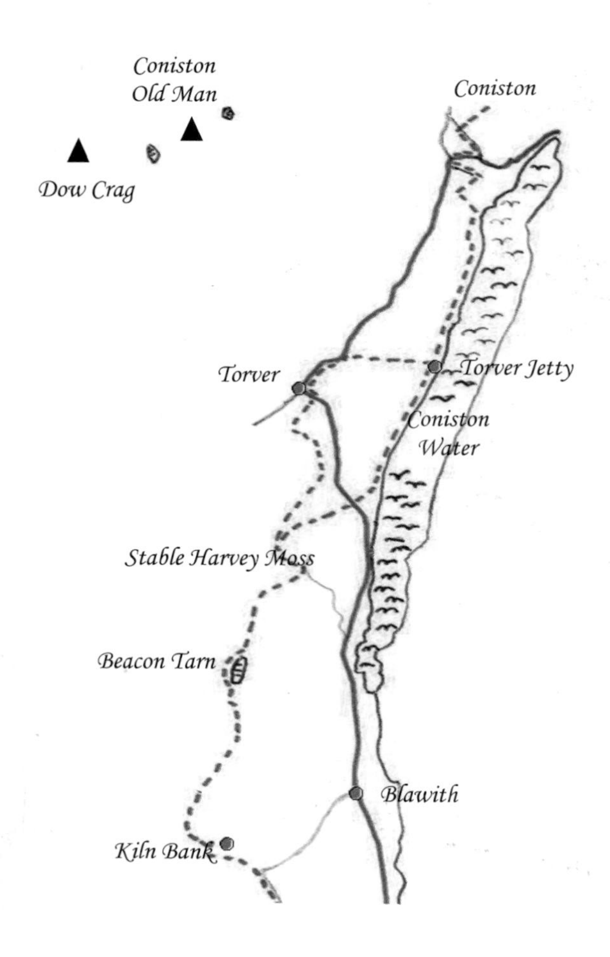

NB In all the "Facilities" tables in this guide, places named in brackets (like Lowick Bridge) are not on the actual route of the CW.

Place	Walk summary
Ulverston	Campsite is at Sandhall 2km SE of town.
Broughton Beck	5.9km from Ulverston to phone box. FPs and quiet roads across farmland. Can be muddy. Phone box is 400m off route. Very infrequent bus to Gawthwaite or Ulverston.
Gawthwaite 5½ mls P.42	8.7km from Ulverston. FPs (possibly muddy) across farmland. Very infrequent bus service to Ulverston.
(Lowick Bridge)	2km from Gawthwaite to Kendall Ground. Low hills and farmland. Generally better underfoot. LB is 2km off rout along quiet roads or FPs from Kendall Gd–see para 1.19
(Blawith)	900m along very quiet road from Kendall Ground to Kil Bank access road. Blawith is 2km off route on quiet roa from Kiln Bank–see para 1.22. *Also Crake Valley camps 1.5km north on main road beyond Water Yeat–see below*
(Birch Bank)	1.1km off route from WMP 300m east of Kiln Bank–see para 1.24. Farm tracks.
Cockenskell	2.8km from Kiln Bank access road. Mostly farm tracks but now in more open country. V good walking from Tottlebank to near Cockenskell.
(Water Yeat)	See Blawith above. Or possible to reach campsite and road via FPs from Cockenskell (see above).
A 5084 near Sunny Bank	4.7km of fell-walking from Cockenskell via Beacon Tarn and Stable Harvey Moss.
(Torver) *(NB also Little Arrow 1.2km north on main road)* P54	2.4km off route from Mere Beck crossing on Stable Harvey Moss at WP 034. (Can also reach Torver from Torver Jetty–see next page.)

CTION 1 OF THE CUMBRIA WAY

B&B etc.	YH/ Barn	Camp-site	Café Pub	Shop	PO	Bank	ATM	Tel box	Bus/ Boat	Train
✓	✓	✓	✓	✓	✓	✓	✓	✓	lots	✓
								✓	509 511	
								✓	509 511	
			✓					✓	X12	
								✓	X12	
		✓								
✓										
		✓							X12	
									X12	
✓			✓					✓	X12	

Place	Walk summary
Sunnybank Jetty	1.5km lakeside walk from A5084. Infrequent launch to Coniston.
Torver Jetty	2.1km lakeside walk from Sunnybank Jetty. Infrequent launch to Coniston. *(Also 2.1km to Torver from here. See entry for Torver on previous page and para 1.41.)*
Hoathwaite	Campsite 600m along lakeside path N of Torver Jetty. Just off route.
(Park Coppice)	10 min walk from lakeshore path just N of Hoathwaite.
Coniston Hall	2km along lakeside path from Torver Jetty.
Coniston	1.6km level walking from Coniston Hall on good paths.

CTION 1 OF THE CUMBRIA WAY (Cont)

NB In all the "Facilities" tables in this guide, the word "In" in the ATM column (e.g. at Coniston) means that the machine is inside (a shop, garage or bar) and will therefore not usually be available 24 hours a day, 7 days a week.

B&B etc.	YH/ Barn	Camp-site	Café Pub	Shop	PO	Bank	ATM	Tel box	Bus/ Boat	Train
									Boat	
									Boat	
		✓								
		✓								
		✓								
✓	✓		✓	✓	✓	✓	In	✓	X12 505 525	

1.1
300m

WP 001

Sculpture at the start of the CW, The Gill, Ulverston

The modern conical structure of metal and stone at the Gill makes an impressive official starting point for the Way.
(WP 001) (E 328488 N 478522 (SD 284785)).

Don't bother fighting the urge to take zillions of photographs of each other (or yourself, if you're on your own), because it'll be nice to look back at them to see how keen and enthusiastic you were at the beginning of your journey.

There are no signposts or waymarks at the sculpture itself, but head just north of west away from the town centre into the narrowing lane to the left of the white-fronted houses shown in the photo. Signs do appear as the lane narrows and runs alongside a stream. Stay by the stream, ignoring any branches off to the right and, about 300m from the start of the walk, come to a signposted junction.
(WP 002) (E 328210 N 478657 (SD 282786)).

1.2
200m

NB Older versions of OS maps show an alternative CW route going straight ahead here. Ignore it.

Instead, turn left to cross a little bridge before climbing quite steeply alongside the edge of the wood. The walled path bends left and then right before bringing you to and through a metal kissing gate as if you were going to walk out onto the road.
(WP 003) (E 328124 N 478597 (SD 281785)).

1.3 1km

Before coming to the road, turn sharp right through a very narrow squeeze stile into a field (CW signpost). In clear conditions you may be able to make out the conical end of the Old Man of Coniston in the far distance; there is also a glimpse of Morecambe Bay from here.

The start of the walk across the fields towards Old Hall Farm. The path stays by the left-hand wall for about 500m

Follow the path easily across two or three fields staying by the left-hand wall. There are good views right to Hoad Hill with its mock lighthouse monument, and ahead to the slopes of Flan Hill. 500m from the squeeze stile, go straight ahead through a gate to join a cart track between fences just where the wall moves away left uphill. You should now be on a broad track heading towards Old Hall Farm and, once there, the path goes straight across the farmyard.

In wet conditions–for example, after a lot of rain or, as when the author was last here, due to a pump breaking down–you might find an unofficial signed diversion asking you to stay away from the yard at Old Hall Farm. If you have to use this diversion, follow the path to the left around the back of the farm. (It is likely to be very muddy here.) The "path" bends right and passes behind the farm area to bring you to a metal gate. Go through this and walk alongside the wood on your left to come to the gap stile at the end of the wood referred to in paragraph 1.4.

1.3 cont

If you don't use the diversion and stay with the official route leave the farmyard by passing in front of the farmhouse. Very soon come to a gated stile on the left with a signpost (that says Cumbrian (with an "n" on the end) Way).
(WP 004) (E 328054 N 479546 (SD 280795)).

1.4 300m

The way out of Old Hall Farm–go left at the SP

Go left through the stile and in 20m go left again over another stile–this one with a waymark post and a CW signpost. Follow the direction of the arrow to walk diagonally across the field aiming for the right hand end of the woodland ahead of you (there is no path on the ground).

Go through a gap stile onto a path that leads uphill. Keep the wood on your left as you climb and, as the incline eases a little, the path moves half-right away from the edge of the wood to go alongside the wall on the right. Do not go through a gate/gap but keep on uphill with the wall to your right. You soon come to a stile in the top right hand corner of the field with another mis-spelt CW signpost.
(WP 005) (E 327851 N 479786 (SD 278797)).

1.5 250m

Over the stile bear right, at first alongside the field boundary. The path swings left to stay left of a monkey puzzle tree and the big house of Bortree Stile.

Go through a gate to cross a green lane just left of Bortree Stile and then go ahead through another gate onto a path in woodland.

The woodland path above Bortree Stile

The path rises alongside a stream and, in 70m or so, turns right to cross it via a little stone footbridge. Ignore a gate on your right and come to a stone through stile in the wall ahead.
(WP 006) (E 327711 N 479951 (SD 277799)).

1.6 350m	Cross the stile and go very slightly right at first. After a few paces bear left around the base of the small hill to head to a ladder stile/hurdle affair.

Over this you're in slightly wilder country–with gorse, bracken and thorn trees–but now on a clear path that leads up through a notch in the skyline to cross another stone through stile. (There are great views back to Morecambe Bay, Ulverston and across to Ingleborough in the Yorkshire Dales.) Now take the obvious way to the house of Higher Lath Farm, passing under some electricity wires on the way and, weather permitting, getting a good view of Dow Crag, Coniston Old Man and Wetherlam–but there's a better one in a minute or two. Cross yet another STS onto a small tarmac road at Higher Lath Farm.
(WP 007) (E 327564 N 480246 (SD 275802)).

The good news is that you have just completed the longest continuous climb on this first Section of the CW: the bad news is that you're about to lose a good part of that height gain straight away. But never mind–the views are great!

1.7 400m	Turn right at Higher Lath and walk down the road. In 400m, come to a couple of houses (Windy Ash) at a bend. **(WP 008)** (E 327896 N 480300 (SD 278803)).
1.8 600m	Go sharp left (signpost) and then straight ahead through a gate onto a green path with a wall on the right.

NB There are no longer any tearooms at Windy Ash: they closed in June 2011.

The Cumbria Way gate at Windy Ash

Pass a couple of barn conversions at Newbiggin and leave this development by the obvious way to soon arrive at Newbiggin Farm. The access road you're on swings away right, but we leave it by going straight ahead (sign on slate) through a gateway into a field with a wall on the right. (The wind farm on Kirkby Moor has now joined the Coniston fells in the view ahead.) Go through another gate and continue in the same direction and come to a STS. Cross this (possibly easy for gymnasts but more difficult for the less agile) and go straight ahead (in the direction you've been following) across the middle of the field to pass just left of an electricity pole. Come to a stile over a fence by a stream.
(WP 009) (E 327769 N 480805 (SD 277808)).

1.9
200m

Cross the stile and the stream but, before you do, take note of the direction that the waymark arrow on the pole near the stile is pointing.

You may be feeling some doubt now, but you need to have faith in the direction the arrow on the post by the stile was pointing. A clear line in the grass heads away half right towards the right-hand end of the roof of the building peeping over the low hill in front of you, **but this is not the way** as it takes you to a gate at the wrong end of the farm, with a polite notice asking you to use the other gate. So, instead, keep straight on (no visible path) up a slight rise and then aim for the left-hand end of the building ahead to come, in about 150m, to a gate at the top (left-hand end) of Stony Crag Farm. Go through this gate (wasn't easy when the author was here last–lift it up!), turn immediately left through another gate, and then right up past a waymarked electricity pole to arrive at a third gate.
(WP 010) (E 327696 N 481026 (SD 276810)).

Approaching Stony Crag Farm.
Go through the gate, immediately left through the next one and then turn right up past the electricity pole to leave by a third gate

1.10
1km

Go through this gate and head across the field with a wall to your right. In 130m, go through a small gate on the right over a stream, and then immediately left to resume the original direction. (There are some possibly confusing WMAs on the gatepost.)

1.10 cont Keep on in the same direction with the stream and hedge to your left and in 200m pass a monkey puzzle tree and a slate CW sign to enter the farm yard at Hollowmire.

Approaching Hollowmire

There are dogs at Hollowmire which bark loudly and seem keen to make your acquaintance. They appear to pose no threat to life or limb however.

Pass the house door and turn right to walk along the farm yard and then leave it onto the access road. (All this is clearly signed.) Walk up the access road to its end and turn left onto the tarmac road at the top.

Follow this road for 300m (there are more views of the Coniston fells and now St John's Church of the parish of Osmotherley as well) and, after passing beneath some electricity wires, the road bends left at a point where there are two metal gates on the right. A few paces further on, across a broad grass verge on the right and hidden by summer foliage (no signpost), is a kissing gate, which is the way we need to go (see photo on next page).
(WP 011) (E 327619 N 481840 (SD 276818)).

1.11
1km

Leave the road by crossing the broad verge on the right and finding a kissing gate hidden in the foliage

Go through the gate (which has a waymark arrow) and bear right towards St John's Church: the path becomes a little clearer and bends slightly left to come to a gate. Go through and head once again towards the church, following a bit of a path just left of a line of trees (ignore the clear sheep track to the right of the trees). The path fades but just aim for the church and, as you approach it, go left to a gate which leads onto a small tarmac road. Turn right and follow the road which bends left just after the church. Come to a junction with a bigger road (B5281) where there is a seat.

Phone box (no coins) 400m down the road to your right.

Turn left and follow this road (take care of fast-moving traffic) for just over 100m, coming to a smaller road going off right to Broughton Beck.
(WP 012) (E 328091 N 482482 (SD 280824)).

1.12
300m

Turn right and follow the road (SP) down into the hamlet of Broughton Beck.

Where the road makes a sharp right turn, leave it by continuing straight ahead down a cul-de-sac road (WM on the road sign) passing left of Barden House. Follow the road as it bends left and, when the tarmac ends, keep ahead, ignoring a footpath going off to the right over a stile.

1.12 cont

Come to a sort of parking area with gates and a stream in front of you. Don't cross the stream but stay with the bigger path that goes left through a metal gate. (WP 013) (E 328329 N 482632 (SD 283826)).

1.13 300m

Take the metal gate on the left. Don't cross the stream

Through the gate stay on the clear track past a newish barn and a new memorial seat (to John Miller). Stay with the left-hand field boundary and pass through two or three gates with that wind farm still on the skyline in front. The field narrows and on the next fence there is a public footpath sign directing you right to a STS in the wall. (WP 014) (E 328144 N 482826 (SD 281828)).

1.14 900m

Bear right as you approach the fence to cross the stile

Cross the stile and go straight ahead away from the wall towards four bushes that turn out to be standing next to small stream. Turn left to follow the stream, very soon crossing it at a little slab bridge. Keep alongside the stream and in 50m cross a stile next to it onto a thin path in a field. Keep the stream just to your left and cross the STS at the end of the field onto a more definite sort of track. The stream moves away left but the way becomes a little clearer as it heads north as an old track with a good wall on the left and a ruined wall and rising ground on the right.

The old track between Broughton Beck and Knapperthaw. When it's not too muddy, all this is excellent walking

About 400m after the STS you arrive at a stile next to a tall WMP. Cross this and join a cart track, keeping ahead in the same direction. The track makes a short climb to join a tarmac road at a signpost.
(WP 015) (E 327957 N 483603 (SD 279836)).

1.15 400m	Go left downhill and in 150m go through a gate into Knapperthaw.

Ignore a public footpath going off to the right, pass the farmhouse and come to a road junction with no apparent waymarks (as at August 2011). Turn right and a signpost will then be seen leaning against the wall in a very relaxed sort of way. In about 130m, just before the road joins another one, go left on grass for 30m and cross the road to reach the big stone pillars marking the entrance to Keldray.
(WP 016) (E 327652 N 483906 (SD 276839)).

1.16
450m

Go down the access road with brilliant views ahead of the Coniston Fells (and with Helvellyn and Fairfield, further right).

The Coniston fells from the Keldray access road

In 400m just after passing through a gate/gap there is a big stone engraved with the word "Keldray" and a small ground level SP with "Footpath" written on it in old-fashioned lettering. Turn left here. Ignore a waymarked step stile on the left but keep ahead up some stone steps to come to another stile that leads out into a field.
(WP 017) (E 327381 N 484219 (SD 273842)).

1.17
850m

Cross the stile and turn right to follow the fence. The RoW stays by the fence to cross a stile but most walkers appear to use the wall gap next to an electricity pole a short distance up to the left.

From the stile (or gap), bear slightly left uphill aiming for a gated stile 30m left of the next electricity pole. After going through the stile follow the wall on your left. In 150m, just in front of some landscaped gardens, the path becomes a track between walls, soon leading past Gawthwaite Farm and so to the main A5092 road. Cross over–and, without fanfare or signs, enter the Lake District National Park–and turn left for a very short distance.

8.7 KM
5 1/2 m/s

NB Phone box (no coins) and a very infrequent bus service here.
Turn right just before the phone box and almost immediately right again to walk down between houses on a small tarmac road. Come to a junction just after Bridge End Cottage.
(WP 018) (E 327174 N 484875 (SD 271848)).

1.18
1km

Turn left (fading homemade CW sign on the wall-end near the gate) and climb very gradually on a narrow tarmac road from where there are good views back over the first part of the route.

Looking back to Morecambe Bay from just above Gawthwaite

This gated road makes for good, easy walking with widening views. Part way along you should get your first glimpse of Coniston Water–a great moment.

An early glimpse of Coniston Water–a champagne moment!

1.18 cont	About a kilometre (15 minutes or so) from Gawthwaite, go through a gate with a CW waymark. There is a wood on the right just here and, in a few paces, having passed the trees, arrive at a junction. (WP 019) (E 327261 N 485788 (SD 272857)).
1.19 850m	Bear right off the main track following the wall to come to, and go through, a gate that has a sign saying "No Vehicles".

You're now on a descending surfaced lane which provides spectacular views towards Coniston and its ring of fells. After 300m, the lane swings sharp right to pass High Stennerley. A hairpin bend to the left takes you away from the buildings and, about 400m after High Stennerley, the lane–now with a tarmac surface and still descending–brings you out over a cattle grid onto a small road. Turn right. In just 20m, before reaching the collection of farm buildings at Kendall Ground, come to a metal gate on your left.
(WP 020) (E 327863 N 486264 (SD 278862)).

NB Escape route here along small roads past Kendall Ground to Lowick Bridge 2km away, where there is a pub/B&B and the X12 bus (for Coniston or Ulverston).

1.20 200m	Go through the gate (signpost) onto a cart track. This soon divides. Take the right-hand branch towards a low hill with thorn bushes.

Take the right-hand fork where the track divides

The track narrows to footpath width and swings right then left round the hill to come in a minute or two to a gate next to a STS.
(WP 021) (E 327845 N 486415 (SD 278864)).

NB There are several gates around here but the one we want is the only one with a stile next to it.

1.21 **150m**	Cross the stile (no waymark) and bear half right on a faint path to cross, in just a few paces, a small stream.

Here bear further right passing to the right of a length of ruined wall...

...and heading slightly downhill towards some bushes, where there is a stout wooden post at a gap.

The post turns out to have a waymark arrow on it. Bear left before the post and head towards a wall 70m away or so. Towards the right hand end of this wall is a stone stile.
(WP 022) (E 327951 N 486573 (SD 279865)).

(From a distance, you may be able only to make out the tall wooden poles next to the stile, not the stile itself.)

1.22 650m	Cross the stile and drop down through trees to a small road. Turn left onto the road and follow it northwards as it climbs gently and winds through a typical south Lakeland landscape of trees and rocks.

On the road to Kiln Bank

In 600m the road makes a sharp right-turn but the CW goes straight ahead, slightly left up the access road to Kiln Bank Farm (marked as Long Lane on the OS map).
(WP 023) (E 327688 N 487098 (SD 276870)).

NB Turning right and continuing with the road here will bring you in about 1600m (one mile) to the main Ulverston–Coniston road at Blawith where there is a phone box and the X12 bus (either back to Ulverston, or on to Coniston).

1.23
350m

Follow the Kiln Bank access road as it descends a little to cross Smithy Beck and then rises towards the farm. In about 350m you pass the farm buildings. Ignore a gate leading to the house and come to a signposted gate in front of you leading into a field.
(WP 024) (E 327352 N 487230 (SD 273872)).

1.24
700m

At Kiln Bank take the gate on the right between the wall and the buildings

Don't go through this gate but turn right through the wooden one in the photo to walk along a short lane between the buildings and a wall to leave Kiln Bank via another gate. Now take the obvious green track that swings left alongside a wall. Soon pass a ruined building and, just over 100m after it, come to a waymark post at a junction.
Fork left for Birch Bank campsite.

Otherwise, go right uphill, still on a clear green track. As the slope eases, the track fades a little but is still easy to follow as it heads on in the same direction (NW) across a spacious, wide open pasture with thorn trees and grey rocks. The path curves right and descends gently to a gate and ladder stile.
(WP 025) (E 327186 N 487700 (SD 271877)).

1.25
550m

Go through the gate. The path becomes slightly clearer as it continues to descend gently, now through bracken and rushes. It soon swings left to run more or less parallel to the wall and then rises to come to a small tarmac road.

1.25 cont

Turn left onto the road and climb towards the enviably situated buildings at Tottlebank Farm, which have been in view since the short climb away from Kiln Bank.

Tottlebank

Before reaching the farm, the climb ends and the road begins to descend slightly just before a left-hand bend where a signed green track goes off sharp right.
(WP 026) (E 327085 N 488203 (SD 270882)).

1.26 950m

Take this track which, although obvious, is not quite where it says it is on the OS map: it is a little further south and east.
(There are two or three places like this on the CW where the route on the ground does not quite match the map.)

The track climbs slightly and then swings left giving good views over the valley of the River Crake–the river running between Coniston Water and the sea–and back to Morecambe Bay. It is superb walking up here, but it is all too brief, as the path soon starts to descend towards Cockenskell. Before it does though, it is worth having a look at the hillside ahead, as you should be able to pick out the path of the CW as it makes its way up to Beacon Tarn.

Looking ahead from the path between Tottlebank and Cockenskell. The onward path to Beacon Tarn can be seen above the conifer plantation

At the bottom of the descent (where our path and the OS version reunite) a track comes in from the right joining ours. Go straight ahead alongside a wall for 60m or so to a place where the path turns sharp left and there is a gate directly ahead of you.
(WP 027) (E 327426 N 488995 (SD 274889)).

1.27
200m

Don't follow the path round to the left but go straight on through the gate onto a field path alongside a wall to your left.

After 100m, the path becomes a walled green lane that leads down to a gate. Go through this, keep left and make a short, fairly steep descent to come alongside a stream. Cross at the little bridge and go through yet another gate–the last one for some time.
(WP 028) (E 327486 N 489167 (SD 274891)).

1.28
500m

There now starts the climb up to Beacon Tarn–the last of the significant ascents on this Section of the CW. This is typical Lakeland hill-walking, albeit on a miniature scale, and is just great.

At first simply follow the clear path through bracken. This soon makes a right-hand bend and comes to a junction with a waymark post. Bear left onto the bigger path. Now it is just a case of going uphill more or less parallel to a wall 50m away to your left. The path winds about a bit but the general direction remains the same (just west of north) and the going gets a bit more rugged as you approach a walled conifer plantation. The wall soon bends away to the left but the path, now very clear, keeps on climbing ahead and you soon arrive at a little col for a fantastic view of Beacon Tarn backed by the now familiar Coniston fells.
(WP 029) (E 327430 N 489621 (SD 274896)).

Beacon Tarn and the Coniston fells from the little col

1.29
900m

Continue ahead on the obvious path to come, in about 200m, to the shore of the tarn just where Tarn Beck flows out from it.

The official CW route takes the left-hand (western) path around the shore of Beacon Tarn. The eastern shore is also do-able and is shorter–but it is rougher and **involves one rocky bit where the path is quite high above the water**. The official western route is easy (but can be very wet, as it stays near the tarn's edge), and both branches reunite just north of the tarn.
(WP 030) (E 327475 N 490412 (SD 274904)).

1.30 1.1km	Climb briefly to another small col and then start the descent towards Stable Harvey Moss.

The path is clear and not too steep. After a short descent, there is a long, almost level section where you walk alongside marshy ground that looks as if it was once the bed of another tarn. At the end of the level section come to a cairn by a thorn tree.

The cairn and thorn tree on the way down to Stable Harvey Moss. See how much closer the Coniston fells are now than when you left Ulverston!

The descent resumes and, after a few minutes, as the gradient eases, the path swings right and becomes grassier under foot.

(*You should be able to see a tarmac road ahead that climbs up left-wards towards a gate. Our route goes almost to this gate, so you can use that as a target–see photo on the next page.*)

As the path almost levels out, come to a Y-junction with a large rock outcrop 80m or so to your left. Bear left here onto the clearer path (no waymark).
(WP 031) (E 327897 N 491373 (SD 278913)).

1.31
550m

The way ahead just after WP 031

Pass right of the outcrop and the path comes to a small stream. Cross the stream and go either up and along the low grassy ridge in front of you or take the smaller path that skirts round its right hand base. Both meet up as the road is reached at a signpost. Turn left and climb the road but for about 50m only, arriving at another signpost just before you reach the gate across the road. Turn left onto a broad track and come, in about 150m to a fork.
(WP 032) (E 328120 N 491753 (SD 281917)).

1.32
600m

The fork on Stable Harvey Moss. The official route goes left to pass the poles, but both branches soon rejoin

Take the left fork and pass immediately left of a double electricity pole before swinging right to rejoin the path you didn't take at that last junction. The path starts to descend gently and soon comes to a junction with a waymark post.
(WP 033) (E 328061 N 492137 (SD 280921)).

1.33
60m

Turn left at this junction

Turn left and, in 60m come to another waymark post at a clear junction near a stream with a couple of small trees.
(WP 034) (E 328029 N 492193 (SD 280921)).

1.34
1km

The Mere Beck crossing. Turn R over the stream for Coniston. Go straight on for Torver

7 mls from Gawthwaite 1.5 mls to Torver

This is Mere Beck, and this junction/stream crossing is the key to the descent towards Coniston Water; it also marks the place where the Torver diversion leaves the main route.

The main route (for Coniston) continues in paragraph 1.34 and the Torver diversion starts at paragraph 1.39.

A decision has to be made here. If you have accommodation booked at Torver, you can use the unofficial Torver diversion described in Paragraphs 1.39 etc. or, if you are still full of beans and want to walk every step of the official CW, you can continue to the path junction at the Torver jetty (see WP 036).(The route to Torver from there is described in paragraph 1.41, and can then be reversed to rejoin the CW.)

The unofficial diversion to Torver from WP 034 may also be useful for anybody bound for Coniston who has had enough walking for one day and wants to finish the journey by bus or taxi, but would prefer somewhere more convivial than a road side to wait for the transport to arrive. Although not a metropolis, Torver does at least have a bus stop, a phone box and a couple of pubs. (You would need to check bus times obviously before committing yourself to this diversion. Please note that the quickest way to a road with a bus route is to walk the half mile down to Sunnybank as described in paragraph 1.34 below.) The Torver alternative is described in paragraph 1.39.

The quickest way to rejoin the CW from Torver is to walk direct to the Torver jetty, this route being described in paragraph 1.40. If you used this route, and took the Torver diversion from Stable Harvey Moss (WP 034), you would replace just over 3km of the official CW with about 4.5km of walking of about the same standard of difficulty. It has to be admitted that you'd miss a couple of kilometres of the lakeshore path, and that there is a short section of main road on the unofficial route, but overall it's quieter and you get the views of the Coniston Fells for a little longer.

1.34 cont

For Coniston (lake and village), bear right to cross the stream. The route continues as a green path which, to start with, is not exactly where it says on the map. In less than 200m come to an unwaymarked junction.

Bear right, staying on the main path, which soon starts to descend the valley of Mere Beck (there is a line of electricity wires over to the right).

An undemanding descent on a path through gorse and bracken brings you to the sturdy footbridge over Torver Beck. Cross this and keep ahead on the obvious path which climbs away from the beck up to the main road A5084. A waymarked track can be seen heading away on the opposite side of the road.
(WP 035) (E 328812 N 492720 (SD 288927)).

Bus for Ulverston and Torver/Coniston.

1.35
2.6km

Cross the road and pick up the track heading away to the right from a small parking space (signposted Torver Commons and Coniston via Lake Shore).

The path climbs gently and swings left before starting a longish descent to the lake shore which you reach exactly at the Sunny Bank jetty (*infrequent launch to Coniston)*.

Coniston Water from near the Sunny Bank jetty

From here to Coniston, it's almost–but not quite–simply a case of following the lake shore. As far as Torver jetty, the path remains quite narrow with several little ups and downs, and with plenty of tree roots etc. to negotiate. After about 1.5km there's a cross wall and you need to be low down near the lake to find the gate through it. Pass right of a wall end and, just before arriving at the Torver jetty (*Coniston launch*), is the path coming in from (or going to) Torver village (the signpost says Brackenbarrow, not Torver).
(WP 036) (E 330065 N 494657 (SD 300946)).

For details of how to reach Torver from here, see para 1.41.

1.36 **2km**	From the junction keep ahead alongside the lake to pass the jetty.

After this the path becomes broader and more level and you are likely to see more people. Just keep on, still in woodland. Pass a University of Birmingham boat place (jetty (Hoathwaite landing)), and go into a field (with camper vans in summer). Stay right and leave this field to come back to the shore from where there are good views left to the Coniston Fells.

Coniston Old Man from the shore path

Pass another path junction for Torver and keep ahead, now in a more park-like environment. Through a gate stay on the broad track which unfortunately leaves the lakeside to take you into a large campsite.

Keep with the track (which may have vehicles on it, so take care) and come via a vehicle barrier to Coniston Hall (easily identifiable from its big circular chimneys). Stay on the obvious (tarmac) way that leads left away from the hall and lake. In 100m come to a gate. **(WP 037)** (E 330389 N 496459 (SD 303964)).

1.37 **450m**	Take the broad track heading right across the field. In 450m or so the path turns sharp right at a junction. **(WP 038)** (E 330213 N 496894 (SD 302968)).

A much thinner path continues ahead across grass to a gate and then half right across a field to the main road. This is a shortcut to the southern end of Coniston village. (There is also a path going off sharp left here which leads to Bowmanstead.)

1.38 **1km**	For the main CW stay with the broad waymarked path which brings you in a further 400m to a road at the entrance to a small industrial estate.

Turn left up Lake Road to reach the main road A5084 close to Coniston's village centre. Turn right to pass a garage and so reach the village centre at the junction with Tilberthwaite Avenue. **(WP 039)** (E 330217 N 497592 (SD 302975)).

Coniston village centre

1.39
2.4km

The Torver Diversion

From Mere Beck to Torver

At WP 034 (para 1.34) where the main (official) route of the CW crosses Mere Beck, if you wish to head for Torver instead, do not cross the stream but keep ahead on a clear path keeping the stream on your right. The path soon swings right to cross the stream and then runs along more or less directly beneath the line of electricity wires. About 200m after the stream crossing, go straight on at a little crossroads, the path now rising gently.

Torver Tarn

Despite the rather intrusive line of electricity poles, Torver Tarn (simply referred to on OS maps as Reservoir (disused)) is an attractive sheet of water in a wild setting and, if you have any spare time, and the weather is kind, you could always consider wandering down to the water's edge for a moment's quiet reflection. If you stay with the path, the tarn and the electricity wires are just down to your left and, as you reach the far (north) end of the tarn, the path drops a little and then climbs ahead on grass. The path is clear throughout with excellent views to Coniston Old Man and his friends as the little rise is crested.

Keep ahead downhill until the walls to your left and right converge to squeeze you through a wooden gate just past a sign saying Torver Commons. The track/lane you're now on leads down to a house called The Mill, pleasantly sited by a bridge over Torver Beck. Do not cross the bridge but climb a track left of the house and through a waymarked gate.

An almost completely unseen waterfall can be heard to your right as this pleasantest of woodland paths heads through another gate and bends left to follow an old hedge/line of thorn trees to yet another gate.

The "pleasantest of woodland paths" on the way down to Torver

Go on ahead between fences with Coniston Old Man now beginning to look much bigger and, after a long turn left, emerge onto a tarmac lane near the entrance to Park Ground Farm.

Turn right onto the lane and at the next T-junction (Moor Farm), turn right again, ignoring the waymarked footpath going ahead across a field (caravan site in the summer season). Follow the tarmac lane with the caravan site to your left to reach the main road at a house and turn left. In 150m or so, you arrive at a T-junction (the A593) which marks the centre of Torver. This is not a WP but the co-ordinates are E 328406 N 494167 (SD 284941).

The Wilson Arms is directly ahead. The Church House Inn and bus stops are a few paces along the Coniston road to the right (you need the left-hand side of the road for Coniston buses). There is a phone box too. The Old Rectory B&B is 750m further along the main road, and B&Bs etc. at Little Arrow are nearly 400m beyond that.

1.40 2.1km

The Torver Diversion
From Torver back to the CW at Torver Jetty

From the T-junction at the Wilson Arms, follow the main Coniston road past the Church House Inn, St Luke's Church (locked, sorry to say) and the village hall. The footway ends here, so you have five minutes or so on the rather busy road. Follow the road as it bends right and crosses a bridge and then turn right through a metal kissing gate onto a public footpath signed Torver Jetty. (It's immediately before Brigg House.) Walk alongside the left-hand field boundary and, where the field ends, follow the fence round to the right for a few paces to cross a length of duckboard over a reedy area. Go straight over this next field to a kissing gate, crossing a long-abandoned railway line en route. Follow the obvious path across the next field, climbing slightly to head left of a low wooded hill. Go through a gate and go straight across a tarmac lane to climb a stony track heading gently uphill (signposted Public Footpath to the Lake No Vehicles No Bikes).

NB if you had been staying at the Old Vicarage or at Little Arrow, you could walk directly to this point along the tarmac lane. You would then have to turn left onto the stony track.

The track winds about a bit and goes past Brackenbarrow Farm, where it levels off. Soon after the farm, there is a junction with two gates facing you. Take the right hand one (yellow waymark arrow). Beyond here, the track narrows to footpath width and starts to descend. Pass through a couple of gates to enter Torver Commons (notice board). The track widens again, steepens and becomes stonier. Ignore any branch paths heading off uphill. Go through another gate and cross a wetter patch and you're in some fine woodland. Go ahead through a gap in a wall and the lake comes into view. A simple walk takes you to the lakeshore. Turn left to arrive, in just a few paces, at Torver Jetty **(WP 036)** (see para 1.36).

1.41 2.1km

The Torver Diversion
From the Torver Jetty to Torver

Approaching from the Sunnybank direction, turn left at the Brackenbarrow signpost just before Torver Jetty **(WP 036)** onto a broad stony path through trees. Reverse the notes in para 1.40.

CONISTON

Street plan (www.openstreetmap.org)

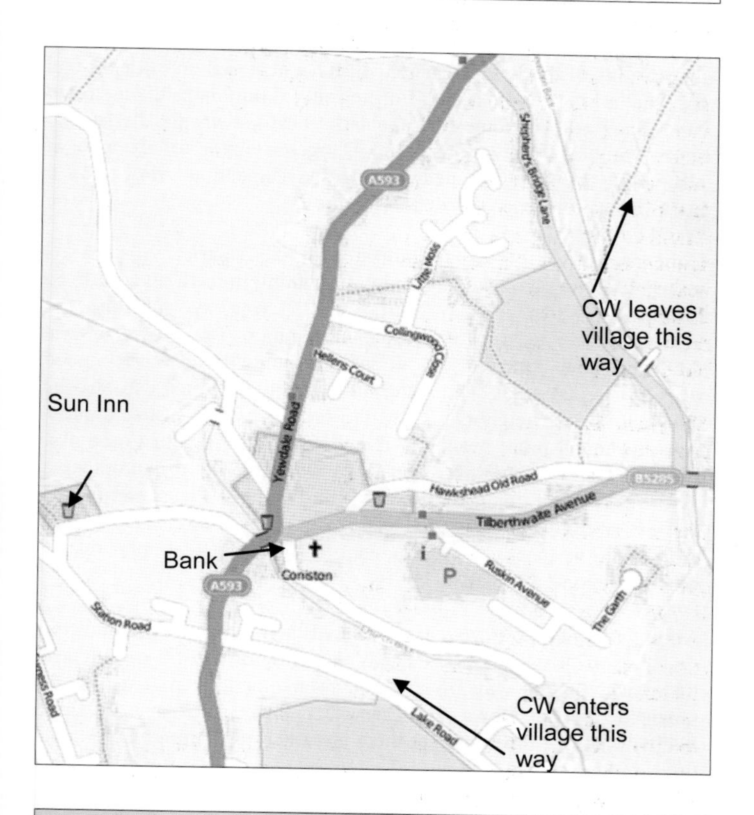

Most of the B&Bs, cafés, shops, pubs etc. are on Tilberthwaite Avenue and Yewdale Road, as are the church, the bank, main bus stop, toilets and the museum.

End of Section 1

SECTION 2: CONISTON TO GREAT LANGDALE (OLD DUNGEON GHYLL HOTEL)

18.6km (11½ miles); 500m (1650 ft) of ascent.

By the time they have completed this Section, any walkers new to the delights of the Lake District, will have acquired an in-depth feel for what all the fuss is about. For not only does this brilliant stretch of walking take in some of Lakeland's best-known and best-loved spots–Tarn Hows, Elterwater and Dungeon Ghyll, for example–it also gives the fortunate pedestrian some stupendous views and a huge variety of scenery to walk through.

Coniston is one of the friendliest of Lake District villages, its industrial heritage of slate and copper seeming to have saved it from twee-ness (if there is such a word) and, if you have the time, the village and its museum are worth an exploration. Tarn Hows, despite the dismissive comments it attracts, is popular for a very good reason: it's just great. The waterfall of Skelwith Force can also be busy but its near neighbour, Colwith Force, is usually just as impressive and much more peaceful. The walk from Skelwith Force past Elterwater and Chapel Stile and on to Dungeon Ghyll is dominated by the ever-more imposing views of the Langdale Pikes, and one of the joys of this Section is that, apart from the pull up to Tarn Hows, the walking is mostly easy. Navigation is also much simpler than it was in Section 1.

Although much more frequently walked than most of Section 1, the first half of this Section (as far as Skelwith Bridge) is not blessed with much in the way of amenity: refreshments can (usually) be obtained at Tarn Hows and Elterwater Park but it is only from Skelwith Bridge onwards that there are all sorts of things to tempt a tired walker–see the "Facilities" summary overleaf.

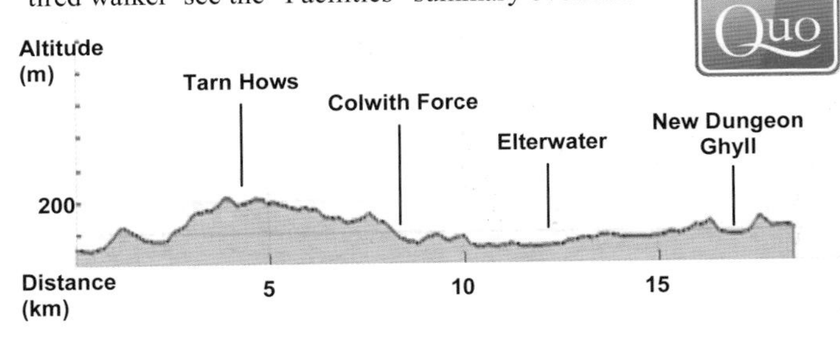

CUMBRIA WAY
SECTION 2
Coniston to Dungeon Ghyll
(Old Hotel)

19km (11½ miles)

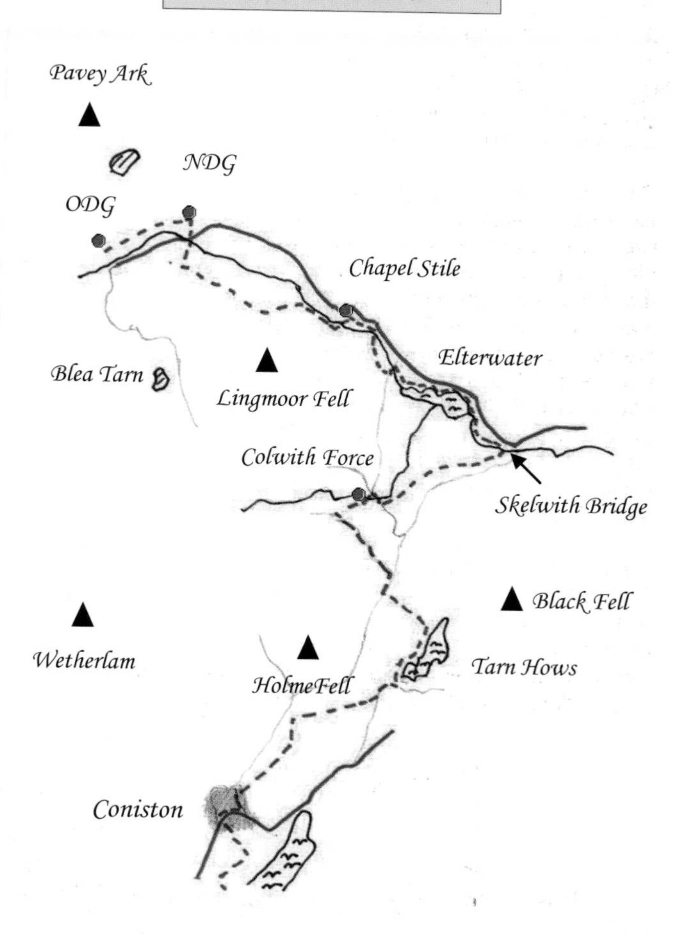

Place	Walk summary
Coniston	
Tarn Hows	4km of good walking ending with climb through woods and along a narrow road. Ice-cream van only (usually).
Elterwater Park (Park Farm on OS map)	5.3km from Tarn Hows. Idyllic walking on good paths and a stretch of narrow road. Tea room/ garden is nearly always open.
Skelwith Bridge	1.2km easy walking on good paths from Elterwater Park. There is no need to use the main road now since the new footbridge was opened in 2007. Facilities at Skelwith Bridge are just off the route of the CW.
Elterwater	2.2km very easy walking on wide path, but subject to flooding in wet weather.
Chapel Stile	800m interesting walk past old slate tips to Wainwright's Inn and 100m further to Chapel Stile village. Baysbrown campsite is on the route of the CW 200m beyond village.
(Robinson Place Farm)	Just over 1km very easy walking on broad paths from Chapel Stile to FB near Oak Howe. Robinson Place B&B 200m off route on good FP.
New Dungeon Ghyll (NDG)	3.5km generally easy walking from Chapel Stile in super surroundings on clear paths. B&B at Millbeck Farm near
Old Dungeon Ghyll (ODG)	1.7km fairly easy walking from NDG on stony, clear pat All brilliant! NT campsite over road.

ECTION 2 OF THE CUMBRIA WAY

tel	B&B etc.	YH/ Barn	Camp-site	Café Pub	Shop	PO	Bank	ATM	Tel box	Bus/ Boat	Train
✓	✓	✓		✓	✓	✓	✓	In	✓	X12 505 525	
	✓			✓							
✓				✓					✓	516	
✓	✓	✓		✓						516	
			✓	✓	✓					516	
	✓									516	
	✓			✓						516	
			✓	✓						516	

As well as its other attractions, Coniston has plenty of shops, a bank and a couple of ATMs. There is nowhere of similar size on the CW before Keswick which is at least two days' walk away, so it would be as well to make sure that you have the wherewithal to get by before you leave.

2.1
550m

From the village centre (**WP 039**–see para 1.39) head down Tilberthwaite Ave keeping the church on your R.

Ignore a turning on the left (Hawkshead Old Road) and walk past the Crown Inn (left) and the TIC, toilets and bus shelter on your right. Ignore another branch of Hawkshead Old Road on your left but, soon after that, about 350m from the start of Tilberthwaite Ave, take the next road on the left. This is Shepherds Bridge Lane and has a road sign for Ambleside as well as a CW waymark. In 200m, having passed the sports centre/playing fields on your right, come to a way-marked footpath going off to the right opposite the primary school. (**WP 040**) (E 330470 N 497812 (SD 304978)).

If you've been staying at any of the B&Bs on Yewdale Road or at the YHA at Far End, you don't need to walk back into Coniston village centre if you don't want to. As the street plan shows, you can approach WP 040 from the other end of Shepherds Bridge Lane.

2.2
600m

Turn onto this footpath which straight away crosses Shepherds (or Shepherd) Bridge.

Immediately after the bridge turn left so that you don't go into the garden of the house in front of you (also called Shepherd (or Shepherd's) Bridge). Take the clear path that runs along the stream for a little way before swinging away right to follow a line of trees. Come to an ornate "folly" which has fairly recently been restored by the National Trust.

There are interesting information boards inside about the building and about the Marshall family who owned this land, as well as Tarn Hows. There are also benches to sit on but, if you've only just started from Coniston, you have to admit that it's a bit early to be thinking about a rest! And, in any case, the sheep might think you've stopped just so you can feed them.

The "folly" on the way out of Coniston

Keep ahead, climbing steadily, to go through a gate, from where there is a good view back over Coniston Water. Continue climbing through an area of gorse. Ignore a thin path branching off right alongside a wall, and soon arrive at a gate where the path leads into a wood.
(WP 041) (E 330791 N 498306 (SD 307983)).

2.3
750m

In not much more than 100m, the path leaves the plantation at another gate and continues ahead, giving good views left to the craggy wall of the Yewdale Fells and the White Lady waterfall, which is really impressive only after a spell of wet weather.

The knobbly little hill in front of you is Holme Fell.

The path becomes a little less clear on grass as it moves slightly right towards a wall with woodland behind it. Just before the wall bends away right there is a waymark post by a boulder just to your left. This directs you to another waymark post by a tree and on through a sometimes muddy gateway. Bear slightly right to walk north-east following the line in the grass across the next field to arrive at a signposted gate by a small wood.
(WP 042) (E 331250 N 498830 (SD 312988)).

2.4
250m

Go through the gate and turn left (signposted Low Yewdale and Tarn Hows) following the stony lane towards the main road.

You soon have Low Yewdale Beck for company and come to a stone bridge on your left. Do not cross it, but go through a gap just to the right of a gate in front of you.
(WP 043) (E 331184 N 499050 (SD 311990)).

2.5
950m

Bear right (NE) across the field following the line in the grass. (The path used to follow the bank of the stream here, but that appears to have been abandoned in favour of the present more direct way.)

In a little over 100m go through a gate into Tarn Hows Wood and follow the now clear path as it swings R away from the stream to climb through trees, soon crossing a small footbridge. In another couple of minutes your path joins/becomes a wider forest track. (The public footpath goes off left near here but has fallen into disuse.) Follow the broad track as it climbs, gradually at first. In about 350m, as it approaches a wall ahead, the track reverts to footpath width, bears right and steepens briefly. There are good views left now towards Fairfield and Helvellyn as the path continues to rise alongside the wall. Go through two gates in quick succession to enter the garden of Tarn Hows Cottage. Follow waymarks and turn right to leave the garden through another gate onto an access road. **(WP 044)** (E 332031 N 499404 (SD 320994)).

2.6
850m

Tarn Hows Cottage, with Holme Fell behind it

Follow the access road as it bends sharp left uphill. In 200m it reaches another road at a gate. Turn left, ignoring both the one-way traffic sign and the bridleway heading sharp left downhill. Walk up the road for about 10 minutes, the reward for your efforts being good views behind and left to Wetherlam and Coniston Old Man. Just after a small long-abandoned quarry by the roadside, you get your first glimpse of the unmistakeable outline of the Langdale Pikes, and these fine hills will become increasingly well-known to you as you continue with your journey. Eventually, you reach a car park (where there is usually an ice-cream van) and, just past it, as the water of the lake of Tarn Hows comes into view, look for a path going off left at a low barrier (CW waymark).
(WP 045) (E 332672 N 499595 (SD 326995)).

The best views both of and from Tarn Hows are from the path going round the right-hand (eastern) edge of the water, but this will take a little longer and it's not the official way: just thought you might like to know, that's all.

And just to remind you that the scene in front of you as you walk down the hill from the ice-cream van is partly man-made. What is now one sheet of water set in conifer woodlands was, until the 19th century, a group of small pools in a marshy wilderness. Some might have preferred it if it had stayed that way, but then they wouldn't have been able to buy an ice-cream here would they?

2.7
1km

Take the path beyond the low barrier and head downhill to the left-hand "corner" of the tarn.

Go through a gate near a bench and cross over the tarn's outlet stream via a small dam. Almost immediately, ignore a path going off left to Glen Mary and simply stay with the wide, very well-walked path for 10 or 15 easy minutes as it winds about a bit and makes one or two ups and downs.

(From point 332881 500035, the path runs closer to the shore than either of the two footpath lines marked on all but the newest of OS Explorer maps, but rejoins them at WP 046). After about 800m of this trouble-free walking, you arrive at an obvious junction sign-posted to Arnside and Langdales.
(WP 046) (E 333067 N 500398 (NY 330003)).

A view of the lake at Tarn Hows from the shore path just before WP 046

2.8
1.5km

Go left at the junction and follow the clear, broad path for 350m to go through a kissing gate next to a padlocked field gate.

Keep ahead/ bear left onto a wider track (signposted Oxen Fell and the Langdales) which undulates gently to join, after nearly 900m (about 15 minutes), the tarmac access road to High Arnside Farm. Follow this downhill for a further 200m to come to the main A593 Coniston–Ambleside road at Oxen Fell High Cross just by a slate-clad cottage called Mole End. Cross the road and, if all has gone according to plan, you will be at a junction with a small road signed High Oxen Fell and with a National Trust Oxen Fell sign just ahead of you. **(WP 047)** (E 332837 N 501771 (NY 328017)).

2.9
450m

At Oxen Fell High Cross. Cross the road and turn right to walk between the wall and the trees

Head right (north) past the NT Oxen Fell sign to follow a footpath between the wall and the woods, with the road just to your right. Soon leave the woods at a kissing gate and keep ahead on grass between an ineffective fence and the wall. The big fells of Helvellyn and then Fairfield come into view ahead. In about five minutes, go through another kissing gate and turn left onto the roadside, which you leave almost straight away to follow a track (with the wall now on your left) to a small road exactly at the point where it divides into two.
(WP 048) (E 332910 N 502216 (NY 329022)).

2.10 900m	Take the right-hand fork (signposted High Park and Hallgarth) and descend with the road to cross a stream.

There is then quite a long climb on the road which, at the top of the rise, bends right to give a great view towards Silver How and Loughrigg Fell (with Helvellyn and Fairfield looking majestic on the skyline). Now descending, the road swings left with a view of Lingmoor Fell and Little Langdale ahead. After 15-20 minutes walk from the A593 road, turn right onto the access track to High Park farm.
(WP 049) (E 332329 N 502846 (NY 323028)).

High Park Farm

2.11
200m

Just before reaching the farmhouse turn right again through a gate with a waymark arrow.

Walk along a level track across a field to go through another gate/gap. In about 100m go through a third gate into woodland. Almost immediately the way divides at a low waymark post.
(WP 050) (E 332487 N 502835 (NY 324028)).

Both branches of the path reunite a little further on, at the road by the River Brathay so, in that sense, it doesn't matter which branch is taken. Older OS maps show the official route of the CW as taking the right-hand fork, which is the Public Right of Way. Newer maps show both options as "official", the left-hand one being on a Permitted Footpath. The left-hand branch visits the waterfall of Colwith Force which, in the author's opinion, is a ***must*** *for anyone walking the CW but, if you've already seen Colwith Force, the other branch makes a very good alternative.*

The original "official" route is described first with the Colwith Force alternative following in para 2.13.

2.12
800m

The Not Visiting Colwith Force Option

Bear right at the waymark post and follow the broad path downhill. In about 5 minutes, you come to a junction at a gap in the ruinous wall to your left. There is a low CW waymark post a few paces ahead of you at this point, and it is worth watching for.

If you miss it, you'll still come out on the right road but will be too far south-east, so will have to turn left along the road to rejoin the correct route at WP 051.

Turn left at this junction, ignoring a narrower path branching even further left, and follow the good path as it winds down through the woods to meet the Colwith Force alternative exactly at a kissing gate and steps leading down onto a tarmac road. Turn R onto the road and in 100m come to a gated stile on the L signposted Skelwith Bridge.
(WP 051) (E 333096 N 502987 (NY 330029)).
Go to Paragraph 2.14.

2.13
850m

The Colwith Force Alternative

At the waymark post at WP 050 turn left. The path descends and swings right to reach the River Brathay and then the top of Colwith Force. The path moves away from the river and takes you down a short flight of stone steps with a fence on your left. A left turn at the bottom of the steps will bring you to a marvellous viewpoint for the falls.

Colwith Force

After a suitable pause for reflection/sandwiches/a brew (or all three), return to the path at the bottom of the steps and continue downstream. The path meanders alongside the river for a few minutes to rejoin the official route at a kissing gate and steps down to the road. Turn right along the road and in 100m come to a gated stile on the left signposted for Skelwith Bridge.
(WP 051) (E 333096 N 502987 (NY 330029)).

2.14
500m

Take the good path across the field and cross a stile to make a steep, stepped climb up the riverbank.

Cross another stile at the top and go on towards the buildings of Low Park. Cross a driveway and go through a small gate onto a continuation of the path, which is now between hedges. Go over a stone stile and cross a rougher field which you leave via another stile. The onward path brings you in 50m to a waymark post just before the buildings of Elterwater Park. Keep on ahead between the buildings soon arriving at the front door of Elterwater Park (called Park Farm on the OS map).
(B&B (all year) and tea garden (or barn, if wet) (nearly always)).

Unless you wish to avail yourself of the B&B or tea room, keep on past the house and leave Elterwater Park through the gate.
(WP 052) (E 333530 N 503220 (NY 335032)).

2.15
1.1km

The broad track swings left, then almost immediately right (signpost Skelwith Bridge).

For 300m or so the easy to follow path meanders through pasture and then takes you past the buildings of Park House via a couple of metal kissing gates. Walk on in front of the white buildings of Park Cottage and Tiplog. In 100m come to a big tree where the path divides. Take the left fork (no WM). In just over 100m the path goes through a gate and starts to descend through trees. Keep left at a waymarked path junction, pass a house called Bridge Howe and arrive at the banks of the River Brathay again. The path soon brings you to the interesting designer footbridge opened in late 2007.
(WP 053) (E 334087 N 503452 (NY 340034)).

2.16
2.2km

The footbridge over the River Brathay near Skelwith Force

Cross the bridge.

For Skelwith Force, the Skelwith Bridge Hotel and pub, Chester's coffee shop, bus to Ambleside or Elterwater/Dungeon Ghyll and telephone box, turn right. Skelwith Force is just a few paces away, and all those other goodies are 150m or so further on.

Otherwise, to continue with the CW, turn left off the bridge, go through a gate and follow the obvious broad track that follows the river. *(The official line, according to the map, goes straight across the big field following a line in the grass; go that way if you prefer– both routes reunite before too long.)* Just as you reach the shore of Elterwater, there is a good view across the lake to the Langdale Pikes.

Unfortunately, this is the last really good view of the lake you'll get on this walk because the path soon enters a wood and the lake is obscured for much of the way. All this section is really very easy– just about flat and no navigational problems. After a little kink in the path, you emerge from the woodland and follow the bank of the stream (now Great Langdale Beck,) all the way to Elterwater village which you reach via a National Trust car park, just by the bridge. **(WP 054)** (E 332777 N 504764 (NY 327047)).
(The map route of the CW does not follow the bank of the stream but adopts a parallel course about 50m away.)

2.17 **400m**

In Elterwater village, the Britannia Inn is just over the green, phone box and public toilets near the car park entrance and bus to Dungeon Ghyll a couple of hundred metres up the road to the right.

Britannia Inn and Elterwater village green

Turn left out of the car park to cross the bridge and then turn right at the white cottage onto a quarry access road (wooden footpath sign with CW waymarks on the wall at the corner). The road climbs gently and in 350m or so comes to a quarry/mine opening on the left barricaded by metal bars. Just opposite this is a signposted footpath heading downhill. Take this path.
(WP 055) (E 332497 N 504989 (NY 324049)).

2.18 **500m**

The path leads you back to the stream before passing alongside some slate tips to come to a wooden footbridge, just before which is a splendid new stone seat.

Cross the footbridge and reach the main valley road just by Wainwright's Inn. Turn left along the road to walk past the pub and, about 50m beyond it, just before arriving at Chapel Stile village, there is a good footpath going off to the left (signposted Baysbrown).
(WP 056) (E 332184 N 505275 (NY 321052)).

2.19 500m

Take this footpath which soon passes round the back of the village school.

Pass a small parking area marked "for School House only" and come to a T-junction of tracks just to the right of a triangular patch of grass. Turn left and then keep right of the buildings at Thrang Farm. Bear right round the cottage of Thrang Garth, and leave down a short, narrow lane between walls which ends at a T-junction with a wider track.
(WP 057) (E 331841 N 505389 (NY 318053)).

2.20 1.3km

The narrow lane between walls on the way out of Chapel Stile just before WP 057

Turn left (away from the village and the main road) and follow the broad track which bends left to cross an arched bridge over Great Langdale Beck. The track then swings right to follow the beck for an easy 800m or so through fields, the first of which is used as a campsite in the season. After a short section where the path and the beck part company, the two come together again at a footbridge. *For Robinson Place Farm B&B, cross the bridge and walk up to the road.* Otherwise, don't cross the bridge but stay with the main track as it bends away left and passes in front of the buildings at Oak Howe. Keep left of the last building (WMP) and then follow the path as it bends to the right and comes to a signposted junction.
(WP 058) (E 330854 N 505762 (NY 308057)).

2.21
1.9km

At Oak Howe, keep on up the valley towards the Langdale Pikes

Take the path going straight on here (SP New Dungeon Ghyll) and just enjoy the first couple of hundred metres of this footpath for what it is–one of the best bits of the whole route.

It is all that a typical Lake District footpath should be: there are old walls, Herdwick sheep, bracken, wild flowers, unexpected twists and turns and fantastic views. If you don't like this kind of walking, then maybe the Lake District isn't for you!

About 350m beyond Oak Howe the path goes through a gate, becomes stonier underfoot and starts to climb gently. This gradual ascent of about 10–15 minutes ends at an old sheepfold just after a stream crossing. The reward for the effort put into the climb (which might be unwelcome if it's late in the day) is the view up to the head of Great Langdale, the big fells of Crinkle Crags and Bowfell having joined the Langdale Pikes on the scene.

Now descend on a clear, partly pitched path and go through a gate to approach Side Farm. Cross the beck over a little footbridge by the farm buildings and walk down the access track to the main valley road with good views of the climbing cliffs of Whitegill Crag directly ahead. Arrive at the main road at a gate with a CW waymark on the adjacent signpost.
(WP 059) (E 329444 N 506312 (NY 294063)).

2.22
500m

Changes were made to the waymarking here in 2012. The arrow now directs walkers left, and then right into the NT car park. Some maps may show the route as going right here, and then going left up the access road to the New Dungeon Ghyll Hotel (NDG) and this is the way the waymark arrow used to point. Although no longer the official route, nor the author's preferred option, the NDG alternative is shown first. Both routes reunite at WP 060.

The Route via the NDG

Turn right along the road for 150m there turning left up the access road to the NDG and Stickle Barn.
Hotel, pub and toilets.
Pass in front of the NDG and keep right of the white painted Stickle Cottage (WM on signpost) to go through a gate into a small field. There is no waymark just here so don't just set off towards the footbridge clearly in view half-right (*unless you want Millbeck Farm B&B*). Instead bear left (line in the grass), pass through a narrow wall gap and come to a junction with a bigger path at a boulder with a metal NT sign (saying Stickle Ghyll) fixed to it.

Pass through a wall gap to a...

...junction with a path at a boulder

Turn right for a few paces only and then go left onto a stony path running more or less parallel to the valley road (i.e. not going straight up the hillside). This makes quite a rough ascent and in 150m meets the author's alternative route at a gate in the left-hand wall. **(WP 060)** (E 329269 N 506494 (NY 292064)).

Go to paragraph 2.24.

The newer route from WP 059

2.23 300m	Go left along the road but almost immediately turn right into the large National Trust car park.

For the new 'official route' (as well as refreshments and public toilets) go right to the far end of the car park. Immediately before the toilets the path goes left through a gap (WMA) and winds right and then left up to the boulder shown in the right-hand photo on page 79. For the author's preferred route however, as you enter the car park look across to the opposite side furthest away from the road and you should be able to see the big grey rock shown in the photo below.

Take the narrow path just right of the grey rock

NB About half way along the left-hand (south-western) edge of the car park, there is a footpath going off through a gate. This is an easier alternative route across fields to the Old Dungeon Ghyll Hotel (ODG), but is not as attractive as the slightly higher way described here. If you really are on your last legs, you might want to consider it though.

Assuming you haven't taken that low-level option, walk just right of the large grey rock and take the thin path that heads uphill into trees. Continue climbing for about 150m to a gate. Go through to rejoin the official route.
(WP 060) (E 329269 N 506494 (NY 292064)).

2.24 900m

Keep left alongside the wall and through the gate ahead, then descend to cross Dungeon Ghyll at a footbridge.

Keep ahead on this excellent path with a good wall to your left and an older, much more intermittent one to the right. There are good views ahead towards the head of the valley, the long serrated skyline of Crinkle Crags being particularly prominent.

Crinkle Crags from the path between the two Dungeon Ghyll Hotels

Pass a stone barn and, about 20 minutes from the NDG, pass behind a white house and then the buildings of the Old Dungeon Ghyll Hotel. At the end of these the CW continues across grass to pass an NT sign for Mickleden.
(WP 061) (E 328521 N 506126 (NY 285061)).

If you want the ODG (hotel/pub and bus stop (516 for Ambleside)), turn left through a gate onto a track that leads past the back of the buildings and round to the entrance.

End of Section 2

SECTION 3: GREAT LANGDALE (ODG) TO KESWICK

24.9km (15½ miles); 650m (2150 ft) of ascent.

The first of the Big Climbs on the CW–the crossing of Stake Pass–is encountered on this Section but, as you can see from the profile, the gradients along the rest of the Section are very easy. Although do-able, the reality is that not all that many walkers do the whole walk from the ODG to Keswick in one day. The reasons for this are connected with availability of accommodation in Langdale and Borrowdale and the wish of most walkers to enjoy the walk and the scenery to the full without having to wear themselves out while they're doing it.

The walk over Stake Pass is grand–a bit of real fell-walking with, as might be expected, some spectacular views. With a height gain of 320m (1,000ft) experienced hill-walkers will know roughly what to expect, while others may not find it quite as daunting as they had feared. Much of the footpath on the Langdale side has been re-laid since about 2008 and the zig-zags and curves have taken a lot of the hard slog out of the ascent. Similarly, work was going on in the summer of 2011 on the Langstrath side to do the same. The approach to Stake Pass along Mickleden could not be simpler–a very gentle walk along a broad track–and the walk down Langstrath is pretty much plain sailing. Also easy is the rest of the journey to Keswick.

Refreshments, public transport and anything else–apart from lots of scenery and quite a bit of gravity–are non-existent all the way from the ODG to Stonethwaite. Thereafter, things get more "civilized" with a good bus service in Borrowdale, three or four pleasant villages to while away some time in and, best of all perhaps, the Keswick launch on Derwentwater which makes a fantastic way to begin or end a day's walking.

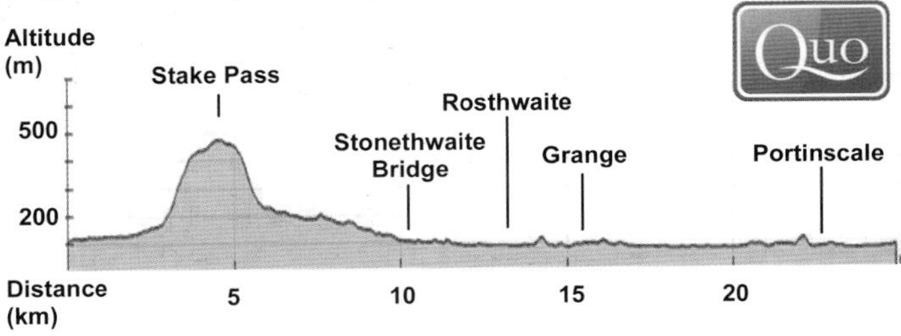

*One of the delights awaiting you on Section 3:
The waterfalls in Stake Beck on the way down into Langstrath.
There are few better places for a relaxing sit down!*

CUMBRIA WAY
SECTION 3 (South)
Old Dungeon Ghyll to
Rosthwaite
12km (7½ miles)

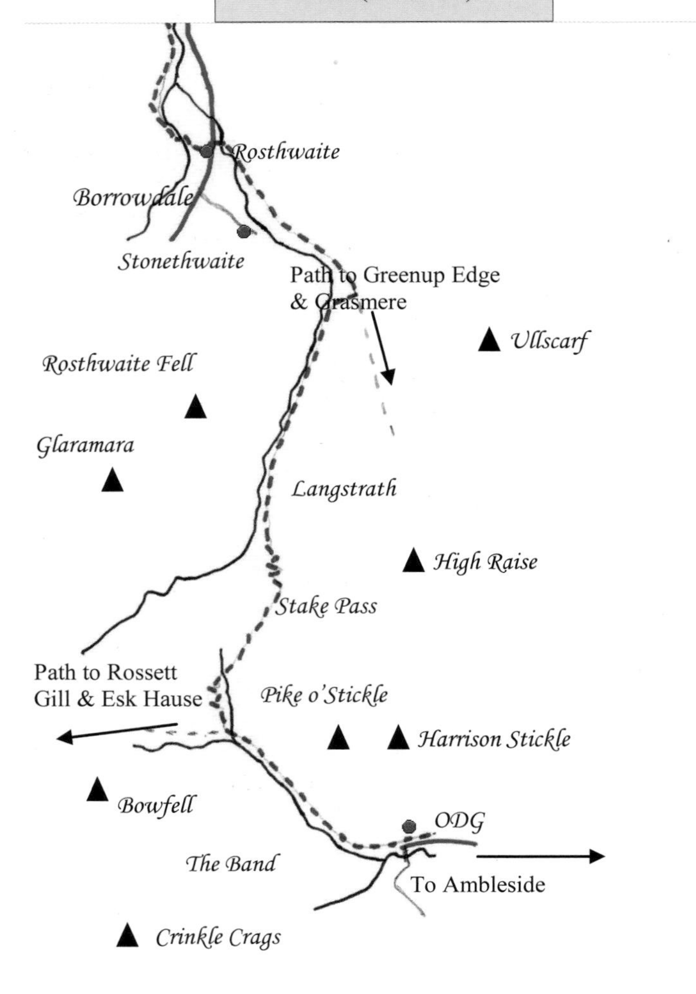

CUMBRIA WAY
SECTION 3 (North)
Rosthwaite to Keswick

13km (8 miles)

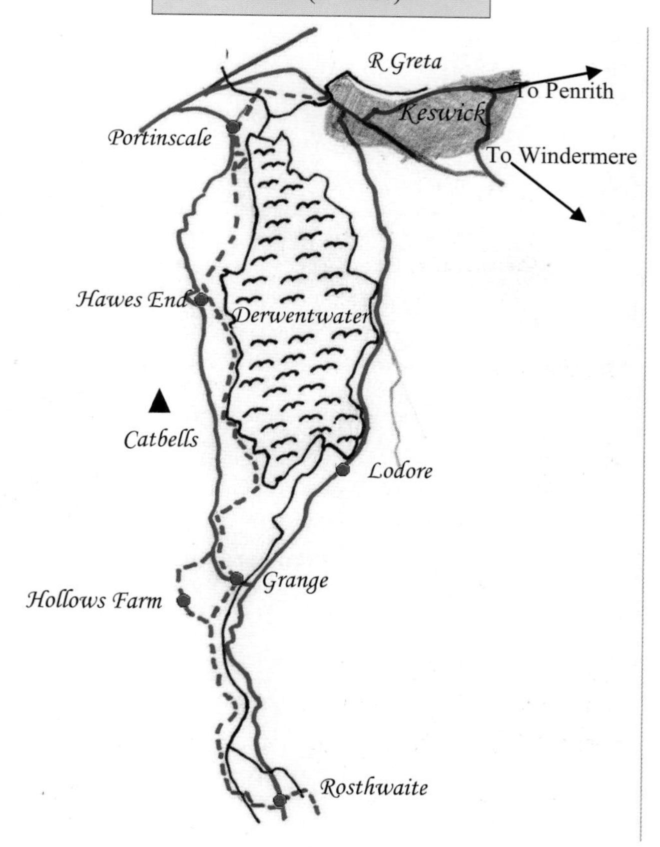

Place	Walk summary
ODG	
Stake Pass	4km from ODG, at first on wide, easy track then a stiff climb up zig-zag path, easing off before summit of pass is reached at 480m (approx). Lots of fresh air and views but no other facilities.
(Stonethwaite)	4km from Stake Pass to FB in Langstrath, giving access to Stonethwaite campsite and village. Further 2.7km to Stonethwaite Bridge, for village. Steep descent at first and then long, easy walk down Langstrath. Good paths throughout. *NB YHA is at Longthwaite 1.1km along roac from Stonethwaite, or it can be reached from Rosthwaite (see below).*
Rosthwaite	1.5km level walking from Stonethwaite Br. (YHA is 1.2km away via a choice of FPs.)
(Grange)	3.2km easy woodland/riverside walking to Hollows Farn campsite. Grange is 500m easy walk off route and Hollo Farm B&B 350m on from campsite on route of CW.
(Lodore)	1.8km easy FP/road from Hollows to shore of Derwent-water. Lodore is 1km E off route on FP partly on raised wooden walkways.
H Brandelhow	1.5km lakeside/woodland paths from Lodore junction.
L Brandelhow	1km idyllic woodland path from High Brandelhow.
Hawes End	700m easy walking from Low Brandelhow, then 200m diversion down to lake or 200m up to road. Catbells Bar 800m off route SW on small road.
Nichol End	1.7km mostly woodland path. May be muddy.
Portinscale	1km from Nichol End–on road all the way.
Keswick	1.8km level walk (roads and field path) to Keswick. *Boc useful only if walking N to S, or just for a pleasure trip.*

:CTION 3 OF THE CUMBRIA WAY

:el	B&B etc.	YH/ Barn	Camp- site	Café Pub	Shop	PO	Bank	ATM	Tel box	Bus/ Boat	Train
			✓	✓						516	
	✓	✓	✓	✓					✓		
	✓	✓		✓					✓	77 78	
	✓		✓	✓					✓	77 78	
										78 boat	
										boat	
										boat	
		✓								77 boat	
										boat	
	✓			✓	✓				✓	77	
	✓	✓	✓	✓	✓	✓	✓	✓	✓	lots boat	

3.1
2.3km

WP 061 The start of the Mickleden track at the NT sign just behind the ODG

If you're starting at the ODG, walk up to the fell path at the back of the building and turn left along this track (the NT sign says Mickleden) (WP 061–see para 2.24). If you're continuing directly from Section 2, just keep ahead across grass to get to the NT sign.

Head west along the broad track, almost immediately passing behind the buildings of Middle Fell Farm. The view ahead up Mickleden towards Bowfell becomes increasingly impressive and you have plenty of opportunity to admire the scenery as there are no navigational problems on this stretch at all: just keep on following the obvious way. Items of interest to look out for include the rock climbers' cliff of Gimmer Crag high to your right and the unmistakeable sugar loaf top of Pike o'Stickle.

Round about where the wall to your left bends away from your track to leave you in open country, you pass beneath the big stony gully spilling down from Pike o'Stickle. This was the site of a Neolithic (4,000BC) axe "factory". The route then crosses the boulder-choked Troughton Beck, identifiable by its little slab footbridge and the V-shaped notch it issues from in the skyline to your right. Not long after this, the path comes alongside the main valley stream (Mickleden Beck) and then you reach and cross a plank footbridge. Just after this is a junction identified by a stone sign with Stake Pass and Esk Hause engraved on it. There is also a cairn and, on the left, a sheepfold. *(Without stops, the walk from the ODG to here should take just over half an hour.)*
(WP 062) (E 326132 N 507373 (NY 261073)).
Make sure you do not miss this junction!!

3.2
900m

WP 062
Plank bridge and guide stone at the head of Mickleden

At the cairn (just after the guide stone), turn right uphill (direction Stake Pass). **Do NOT go straight ahead on the bigger path towards Esk Hause/Rossett Gill.** The ascent of Stake Pass is the toughest ascent on the CW but is, in reality, not too bad. The recent work on the footpath has made following the original zig-zags much easier than it used to be, and you might be surprised to discover how much less steep the path is than it looks from below. Then again you might not! It's still quite hard work though, and you will probably have plenty of opportunity to stand and admire the views: the one looking back down Great Langdale with Pike o'Stickle dominating the foreground is especially striking, but they're all good. Just take your time and make the most of the scenery.

Looking back to Pike o'Stickle and Mickleden from the path up Stake Pass

3.2 cont	Also attractive are the little waterfalls in Stake Gill which the zig-zagging path comes close to from time to time. Almost exactly as the steepness eases, the path comes to and crosses Stake Gill. **(WP 063)** (E 325999 N 508168 (NY 259081)).
3.3 800m	Continue ahead on the clear path, which is much less steep now, but still rising as it heads for the top of the pass.

The route now enters a strange landscape of hummocky moraines (small grassy hills left by glaciers during the last Ice Age) and the path winds about a bit with one or two small descents to interrupt the generally rising nature of the walk. Just before the top of the pass is reached (10 or 15 minutes' walk from the stream crossing), a clear path goes off very sharp right. This heads south and is the way to the Langdale Pikes. It is NOT our route. In clear weather there will be no difficulty but the junction might cause some doubt in bad weather. Just remember that the CW does not head south at any point between the stream crossing and the summit of the pass. Immediately after this junction is a boggy patch crossed by some large boulders, then a smaller turning left (which you also ignore) and then the summit cairn, all these things occurring in the space of less than 50m.
(WP 064) (E 326524 N 508699 (NY 265086)).

WP 064

The summit of Stake Pass (Skiddaw in the distance)

3.4
500m

Walk past the cairn and keep straight on, just west of north for a few paces until you've passed a large pool/ small tarn on your left, then just east of north as the now smaller path descends gently.

The path does fade from time to time in marshy areas but is generally easy to follow. If in doubt, you should have gently rising ground to your left while to your right the ground falls away equally gently to the stream (Stake Beck). 500m from the summit cairn, you come to a sudden steepening of the slope from where, in clear weather, you get a dramatic first view of Langstrath. This point is the key to the descent.
(WP 065) (E 326706 N 509183 (NY 267091)).

3.5
850m

The first view down Langstrath from near WP 065 (Skiddaw in the far distance)

As at July 2011, much footpath repair work continues to be done to the path on this side of Stake Pass. The old luxurious zig-zags had, over the years, been savaged by short-cutters, and the advantage of the newly laid path is that all walkers will, in future follow a single well-built trail up and down the fellside. The downside is that, in the short-term at least, the lines of the new path are harsh and have not yet blended in to the landscape, but they should do in time: in any case the waterfalls of Stake Beck are cheerful company almost all the way down into the valley bottom. As the foot of the slope is approached, the path fades in wet grass, but the way down is pretty obvious. The target is a footbridge that you can't see (although you could from further up the slope) so head for a lone tree that acts as a reliable guide until the bridge comes back into view.
(WP 066) (E 326485 N 509823 (NY 264098)).

3.6 3.4km	Cross this bridge, but not the one 150m away half left.

Keep ahead following a clear path along the right-hand side of the valley floor for the next three and a half kilometres or so. Langstrath is claimed to be the longest uninhabited valley in the Lake District and the name itself means "long valley". Some people say it is bleak: it's certainly wild and unspoilt and it's a joy to walk down. After about 1500m, the path reaches a wall which it crosses by a ladder stile (or there's a gate a few paces away). Another gate immediately afterwards brings you to an area of damp ground to your left. If you pick a way across this you'll come to Blackmoss Pot, a deep diving pool in Langstrath Beck. It's certainly worth a quick look, but be aware of the sudden vertical drop into the water. Keep hold of children and dogs (if you have them with you of course–there's no need to go and find any specially).

Blackmoss Pot, Langstrath with Bowfell in the background

The big outcrop of pale grey rocks you will have seen on the other side of the valley just before coming to Blackmoss Pot is Cam Crag, one of Lakeland's most popular rock scrambles.

After returning to the path, just keep on keeping on, staying on the main path. Less than 200m from Blackmoss Pot, the path threads its way through a chaotic jumble of tumbled boulders, with the enormous Blea Rock (or Gash Rock) prominent up to your right. In a further 400m pass through a wooden gate, from where you can get a good view back to Bowfell.

Looking back to Bowfell from Langstrath

The path gets easier–but a little wetter–as you reach a footbridge on your left (*access for Stonethwaite campsite*). Unless you want the campsite don't cross this bridge, but keep ahead with the stream still to your left. Go through a small gate so that you have a fence on your right and come to an attractive place by the stream where there are little waterfalls to look at and where there is a massive choice of comfortable flat stones to sit on. They look to have been designed especially for tired walkers to rest on while they watch the world not going by so, if you're not in a tearing hurry, why not take advantage of them? Cross the footbridge over Greenup Gill which combines with Langstrath Beck just here to form Stonethwaite Beck, and climb a few steps to go through a gate and so join the track coming down from Greenup Edge to your right.
(WP 067) (E 327439 N 512999 (NY 274129)).

3.7 1.4km	Through the gate, turn left onto a clear track which you follow all the way to Rosthwaite, less than 2 miles away.

The way is obvious just about all the way and is easy Lake District walking at its best. Lots of trees for shade (or shelter) but still enough open space to offer views of the surrounding hillsides. Especially worthy of note is the impressively vertical cliff of Eagle Crag which can be seen in profile if you look to your right as you go through the gate at the junction of Langstrath Beck and Greenup Gill.

Looking back to Eagle Crag from the Greenup junction

Route-finding is no problem although there is just one place, immediately after a footbridge, where the path appears to split. It doesn't matter which branch you take, but the right hand one is on grass which is luxury for tired feet after all the stones you've trodden today. About 1.4km (20–25 mins) from WP 067 you pass through a gate and come to an obvious signposted junction.
(WP 068) (E 326406 N 513862 (NY 264138)).

Turn left to cross the bridge for Stonethwaite village–B&B, campsite, pub, phone box.

3.8 1.5km	To stay on the CW go straight ahead (north-west) soon enjoying wider views of the valley of Borrowdale.

Looking ahead down Borrowdale from the CW between Stonethwaite and Rosthwaite

The track winds about a bit but is never in doubt. After a short section alongside Stonethwaite Beck you arrive at a signposted junction where a left turn onto a cart track takes you over a bridge to join the main valley road B5289. Turn left, pass the bus shelter (*bus to Keswick*) and almost immediately come to a junction on the right just before reaching the "Narrows" in the village of Rosthwaite. **(WP 069)** (E 325839 N 514904 (NY 258149)).

The Narrows in Rosthwaite. The CW takes the lane on the right. Scafell Hotel (and pub) etc. straight on between the houses

3.9
950m

Rosthwaite has hotel/pub, B&Bs, tea room, phone box, toilets and buses to Keswick and Portinscale.

To continue with the CW, turn right up the tarmac lane and pass a phone box, toilets, an NT car park and the village hall and then go between Yew Tree Farm (B&B) and the Flock Inn tearoom. The lane continues, now without a tarmac surface, to arrive, in 300m, at the river. Turn right with the track and walk a further 300m to cross the stone bridge (New Bridge). Turn right off the bridge and in less than 100m come to two gates in front of you.
(WP 070) (E 325148 N 515180 (NY 251151)).

3.10
1km

Go through the right-hand gate. In about 200m the easy level path comes to a fork just in front of a wooded knoll.

The official route and the right of way go right here, but this path could be difficult if the river level is high. So, do as nearly everybody else does and take the left fork. Ignore a gate and stile leading away left up the slopes of Castle Crag and enter woodland at a gate. It has been said that, even if it had no hills and no lakes, the Lake District would still be worth walking in because of its trees, and this walk through High Hows Wood is a fine example of that.

The CW in High Hows Wood, Borrowdale

After 500m (7 or 8 minutes) of this excellent woodland walking, go through a wall gap into an area of old quarry spoil heaps. Ignore a smaller path branching off left and climb a little to a T-junction with a signpost.
(WP 071) (E 325198 N 516074 (NY 251160)).

3.11
700m

WP 071

The junction with the SP just after the quarry tips

Turn right, still on a very clear path. This descends gradually for 200m or so to go through a wall gap where it turns right and drops a little more steeply to river level. After a level section near the river and with the valley road in view on the opposite bank, there is a short rise up to a gate and stile (as well as a nice bench to sit on). Drop down again towards the river and come to a junction with the path to Seatoller (SP).
(WP 072) (E 325062 N 516527 (NY 250165)).

3.12
500m

Bear right to go down to cross a couple of streams– hopefully you won't need to use the footbridges, but they're there just in case.

The track briefly comes back to the riverside, but leaves it again almost immediately to lead up to join the access track to a campsite. Bear right along this broad stony track which has a wall to your right and in 300m come to a gateway.
(WP 073) (E 324983 N 516992 (NY 249169)).

For Grange village (tea rooms, toilets, bus to Keswick and Portinscale), keep ahead and turn R onto a tarmac road for 500m. To rejoin the CW, either retrace your steps or just follow the road (west and then north) for 350m to the Borrowdale Gates Hotel where the official route comes down to the road through a gate.

3.13
350m

WP 073 The CW goes L here. For Grange, keep ahead and then turn R

To stay with the CW and miss out on Grange, bear left immediately after the gateway onto a slightly smaller track and go left again onto the access road to Hollows Farm. Go straight through the farmyard and leave it through a gate at the right hand side of its far end. Keep ahead to cross a small field and walk up to leave the farm area through a gate. **(WP 074)** (E 324752 N 517249 (NY 247172)).

3.14
1.3km

Follow the broad, gently rising track for 350m until it arrives at a wall forming the boundary of a plantation (High Close).

Turn right and go through a waymarked gate onto a small green hill called Peace How (not named on OS maps). The path heads right keeping right of a holly tree, but it is worth the 1 minute climb to the little summit where you can enjoy a tremendous view and a luxurious sit down on a slate seat.

Rejoin the path and follow its winding way down to the road at the Borrowdale Gates Hotel. (*This is where this route and the Grange alternative reunite: turn right for Grange–cafés and bus)*. Otherwise, turn left onto the road and follow it for 600m (7 or 8 minutes). This road has no footway and carries a fair amount of traffic, especially in the summer. Just after crossing a stream (Ellers Beck) and with the buildings at Manesty clearly in view ahead, come to a signposted gate on the right.
(WP 075) (E 325104 N 518257 (NY 251182)).

3.15
500m

Follow the broad path across the field (with views of Catbells–one of Lakeland's favourite summits–to your left) and leave it through a kissing gate.

The path runs alongside a walled wood/caravan site for 150m or so and brings you to another gate.
(WP 076) (E 325426 N 518636 (NY 254186)).

3.16
1km

Go through the gate and, in a few paces, bear left at a junction. (*A right turn will bring you in 1km to Lodore on the main road–hotel and bus/launch to Keswick.*)

Very soon cross a short plank bridge across a boggy area, immediately after which bear right to reach an obvious made FP. Turn left and follow the easy, level path as it meanders about a bit, dodging wetter ground (sometimes on duckboards) and enters Manesty Wood through a gate. The path remains easy to follow and comes almost to the lakeshore at Abbot's Bay, from where there are good views across the water towards Skiddaw and Blencathra. Soon after this you arrive at a house called the Warren.
(WP 077) (E 325154 N 519324 (NY 251193)).

3.17
1km

Turn right and follow the lane gently downhill to arrive in 100m at a junction where there is a stone seat (marked Irene's View) and a great view across the lake.

The view across Derwent-water from Irene's View.

3.17 cont

Bear left and go through a gate with a white house in front of you.

Pass between the house and a wooden garage, and then go right again through another gate to walk around a headland apparently composed of mine waste. Soon after re-entering the wood keep low (right) at a fork to pass the High Brandelhow launch landing stage (*launch to Keswick*).
(WP 078) (E 325171 N 519774 (NY 251197)).

3.18 1km

WP 078 The landing stage at High Brandelhow on Derwentwater

Assuming you have spurned the chance of a boat ride, just keep on along the easy but wonderful path through the woods by the lake shore. In about 800m you reach a pair of giant wooden hands, an installation entitled "Entrust", which celebrates the centenary of the National Trust in 2002, this western shore of Derwentwater being where it all started. 200m further on, you reach the Low Brandelhow landing stage (*launch to Keswick*) and leave the wood through a gate.
(WP 079) (E 325238 N 520716 (NY 252207))

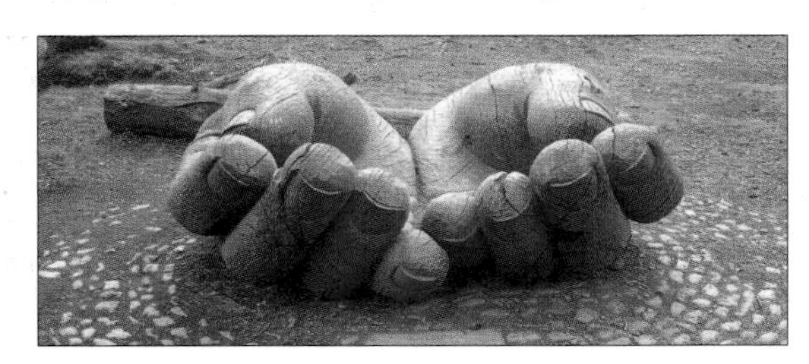

3.19
750m

Turn left away from the lake on a clear path which soon passes through another gate and swings right to pass a small sign saying that you're on the path to Lingholm and Keswick.

Go through a metal gate, pass an interestingly carved fallen tree trunk (another NT celebratory piece) and rise up to join a small tarmac road. Bear right to pass the Hawes End Outdoor Centre and come to a small path heading downhill (SP Landing Stage). (*Another chance of a boat to Keswick.*) Unless you want the boat, don't take this path but keep ahead and very soon come to a junction with a SP. **(WP 080)** (E 324860 N 521370 (NY 248213)).

3.20
1.2km

WP 080 The CW goes through the small gate arrowed. (Go L uphill at the SP for the bus to Portinscale and Keswick)

Walk a little way past the junction (where there is a footpath climbing left towards Catbells and the road for the bus to Portinscale and Keswick, and an unsigned tarmac road going off right), and take a kissing gate on the right (SP Lingholm and Keswick). The woodland path descends through a dark rhododendron tunnel, crosses a little bridge and emerges into a clearing. Follow the clear path across the field, from where there are good views back to the knobbly top of Causey Pike and to Catbells. Re-enter woodland at another gate and, again, follow the obvious path which, in 650m, comes to the access road to the big house of Lingholm. Go straight across onto a wider path with a wall on the right (signpost to Keswick) and in a short distance come to a fork with a waymark post.
(WP 081) (E 325200 N 522378 (NY 252223)).

3.21
1.3km

WP 081 The WMP just beyond Lingholm. Either fork is OK, but the RH one goes to Nichol End (launch and café)

You have a choice here, both options now being waymarked as the CW. The “traditional” way is to go straight ahead, slightly uphill through trees. The path soon levels out and then descends, quite steeply, to emerge via a gap in a hedge onto a tarmac road where you keep ahead in the same direction, very soon coming to the junction with the Nichol End access road.

The alternative, which is easier, is to turn right at the waymark post following the wall downhill. In a few minutes, pass a house with a gated porch and come to Nichol End, a busy little place with a nautical sort of feel to it. There are yachts and a marina and, probably more relevant to most Cumbria Wayfarers, a café and a final chance of taking a launch to Keswick. Assuming you resist this last temptation, just take the access road away from the lake and, in 150m, rejoin the other route at the road-end.

Keep ahead (if you came over the hill), or turn right if you’ve come from Nichol End and follow the roadway into the village of Portinscale. (There is a footway for much of the way, but you will have to cross the road once or twice to make use of it.) There is a good view of Skiddaw straight ahead. *In the short distance between the Nichol End road and Portinscale you will pass three cafés/licensed bars: Derwent Bank, the Derwent Lodge Hotel, and the Portinscale Tearooms.* Just after the tearooms the main road bends away left (signposted Keswick for road traffic) and on the right is the former hotel of Harney Peak (now split into apartments).
(WP 082) (E 325214 N 523546 (NY 252235)).

3.22
1.8km

Keeping left with the main road will take you to most of Portinscale's B&Bs as well as the Farmers Arms pub. You can also get a bus to Keswick from here, but it hardly seems worth it now–you're nearly there!

Immediately after Harney Peak, turn right onto a smaller road to walk past the Derwentwater Hotel and then the Derwent Hill Outdoor Centre. At the end of the road continue ahead across the bouncy suspension bridge over the River Derwent.

Skiddaw seen from the suspension bridge at Portinscale

After the bridge, keep on for a short way along a stretch of cul-de-sac road often used as a car/coach park (or, better, use the small field just to the right). In 150m turn right through a signposted gate and follow the fenced footpath for 800m across fields to the Greta Bridge in Keswick. For the town centre, bus station and most of the eateries, cafes and accommodation providers in Keswick, turn right and cross the bridge. Keep straight ahead at a mini-roundabout (*right turn for bus station*) and straight on again into the market place where the main road bends away left. Walk up the market place to come to Keswick Moot Hall (TIC).
(WP 083) (E 326635 N 523420 (NY 266234)).

As well as housing the TIC, the Moot Hall is right in the centre of town so is convenient for nearly all the goodies Keswick has to offer. The route notes for Section 4 of the CW start from the southern end (i.e. not the clock-tower end) of the building as if you were starting with your back to the TIC door.

Keswick is the '"capital" of northern Lakeland and has just about all the amenities you could wish for. There are loads of shops (including two supermarkets–Booths and a Co-op), banks, ATMs, a Post Office, reasonable bus services to Penrith (for the train), Windermere, Carlisle, and many local places. There are not many places between Keswick and Carlisle that have an ATM or a bank so, if you need cash, get it here.

There are also restaurants to suit all tastes, a cinema, a theatre and two or three good museums. Not bad for a small town.

KESWICK
www.openstreetmap.org

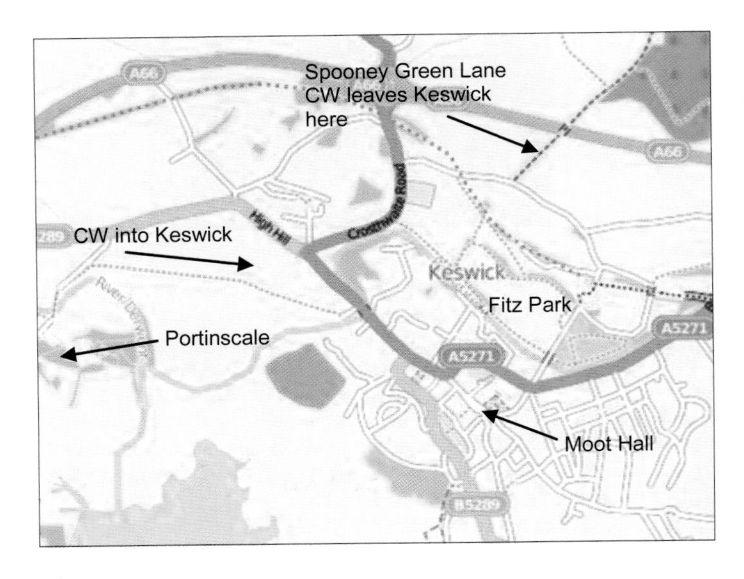

KESWICK CENTRE

(showing main area for B&Bs)

www.openstreetmap.org

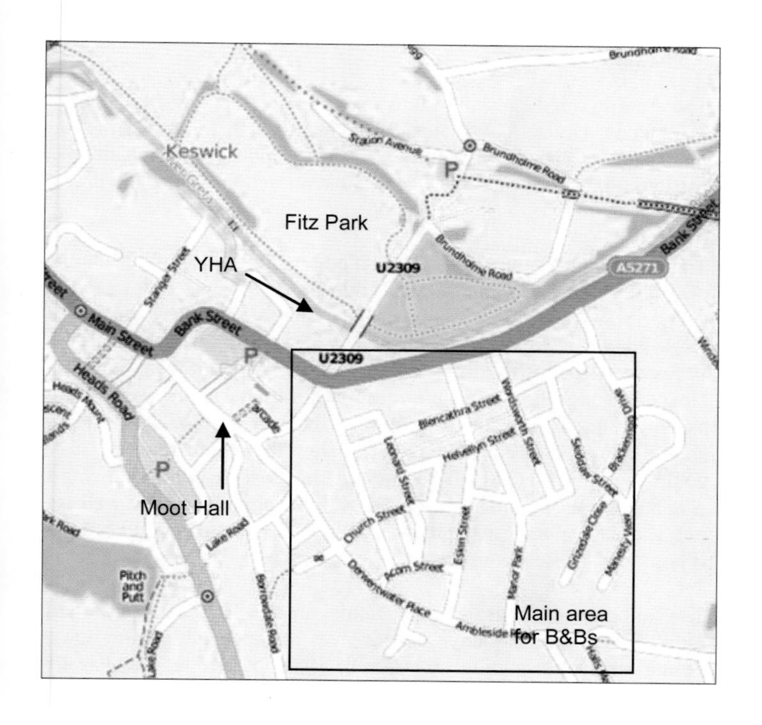

End of Section 3

SECTION 4: KESWICK TO CALDBECK

24.2km (15miles); 900m (3000 ft) of ascent (Eastern Route via High Pike) or
29.1km (18miles); 900m (3000 ft) of ascent (Western Route via Orthwaite).

There are two recognised options on this stage, the first 9km (as far as Skiddaw House Youth Hostel) being common to both, as is the final short stretch from Nether Row to Caldbeck. It's the middle sections that differ and both have their attractions and their draw-backs.

The usual route is the shorter eastern one, which takes in the summit of High Pike. At 658m (2157ft) this is the highest point on the Cumbria Way and is the only actual fell top visited by the route. High Pike is a great viewpoint and is a rolling, grassy hill with a very easy descent towards Caldbeck. But the way to it from Skiddaw House is long and fairly unfrequented, with the main part of the ascent being without major paths. In fine, clear weather the walk should not pose any problems but, in low cloud and rain, the way could be confusing and, after a prolonged wet spell, some of it could also be unpleasant underfoot. It is usually recommended that walkers not confident in their navigational skills should leave this route alone if poor weather seems likely.

The alternative route via the fields around Bassenthwaite and Orthwaite is 3 miles longer and involves just as much up and down as the High Pike option so, overall, is no easier. It, too, has its navigational puzzles, but they are at farmland level, so will not involve floundering around on an exposed hillside. They are also avoidable at the price of a little road walking. The highlights of the western alternative are Dash Falls–which, after rain, are one of Lakeland's finest waterfalls–and the excellent track that runs around the north-western flank of Longlands Fell.

Looking back to Skiddaw House from the River Caldew on the main route

Little Tarn near Orthwaite on the western alternative route

Whichever route is chosen, accommodation before Caldbeck is scarce, and places of refreshment actually on the route are non-existent. If you're doing the High Pike route, you could consider breaking the stage into two by making the diversion to Mosedale village where there are a couple of B&Bs. To rejoin the route you would then have to walk back to Carrock mine for the ascent of High Pike, or you could use small roads and lanes to reach Caldbeck that way. Lingy Hut high up on High Pike offers very basic shelter–camping in a wooden shed rather than under canvas. On the western route, things are not a lot easier–Bassenthwaite (a mile or so off route) offers some B&B accommodation (and there's a pub) or you could walk down to the main road from Peter House Farm and get the bus back to Keswick, reversing that journey the following morning.

NB Collection and return service from Peter House (and Caldbeck) may be possible from Strand Bank B&B at Sebergham.

Apart from the somewhat sketchy bus service from Bassenthwaite or High Side to Keswick, there is the infrequent Caldbeck Rambler service connecting Mosedale with Hesket Newmarket and Caldbeck. Public telephones are also very infrequent on this Section, and there are long stretches with no mobile phone signals, especially in the Skiddaw House area.

Whether you choose the main route or go for the Orthwaite alternative, some of the walking is along easily-graded paths across wild and unfrequented territory. Nowhere else on the CW is likely to offer such peace and solitude.

Eastern Route via High Pike

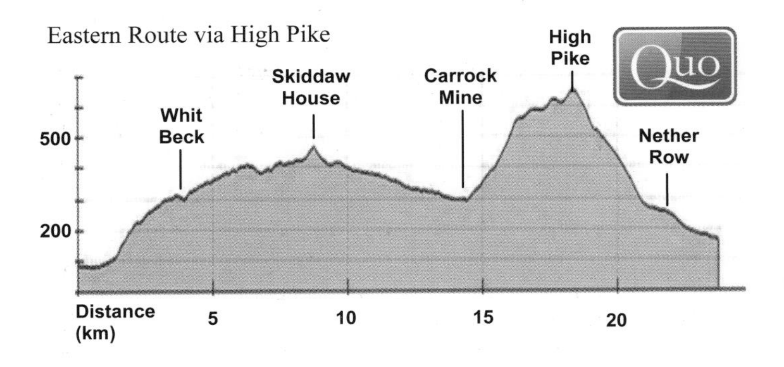

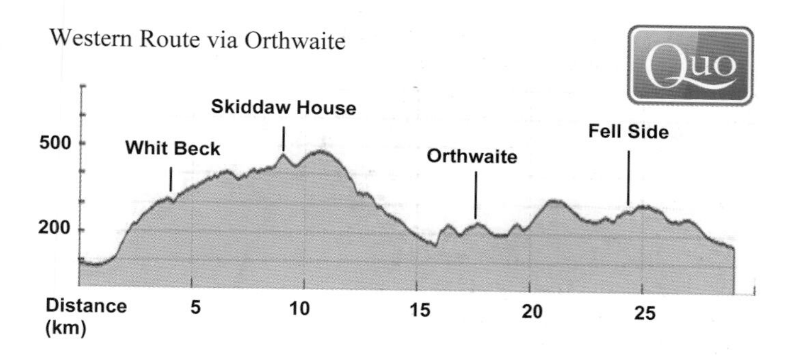

Please read! Rogue birdlife on the Orthwaite Alternative!

The 2.5km (mile and a half) of the official route from Peter House to Orthwaite is scenically pleasant enough (and you do get to see the very shy Little Tarn) but; navigation isn't all that straightforward, there are cattle about, there is one steep, though short, ascent and, most importantly, there is the Buzzin' Buzzard of Orthwaite.

This is not a joke!! The author has been dive-bombed and threatened by this aggressive character three times, and research has revealed more evidence that this bird does not like walkers encroaching on his territory. There are reports of attacks on other people over the last three or four years, and being in a group is no guarantee that he won't attack. He has even drawn blood on occasions. I am assured that the bird is dangerous and is a well-known local menace! The area he patrols is roughly from above Little Tarn to the road at Orthwaite (paragraphs 4.23 and 4.24), and he is thought to attack only in spring and summer. This warning is not intended to dissuade you from taking the official route but, as this claims to be a comprehensive guide book, you'd better have all the facts. If you do decide to go for it, the author's advice is to have your head covered, keep your eyes open and go armed with walking poles or similar: waving these above your head may keep him at bay.

The alternative is to turn right at Peter House and follow the road to Orthwaite a little less than 2km away. It's easier and safer–unless you get hit by a car of course–although admittedly it's not strictly "doing the Cumbria Way". But, hey...

CUMBRIA WAY
SECTION 4 (South)
Keswick to Skiddaw House
9km (5½ miles)

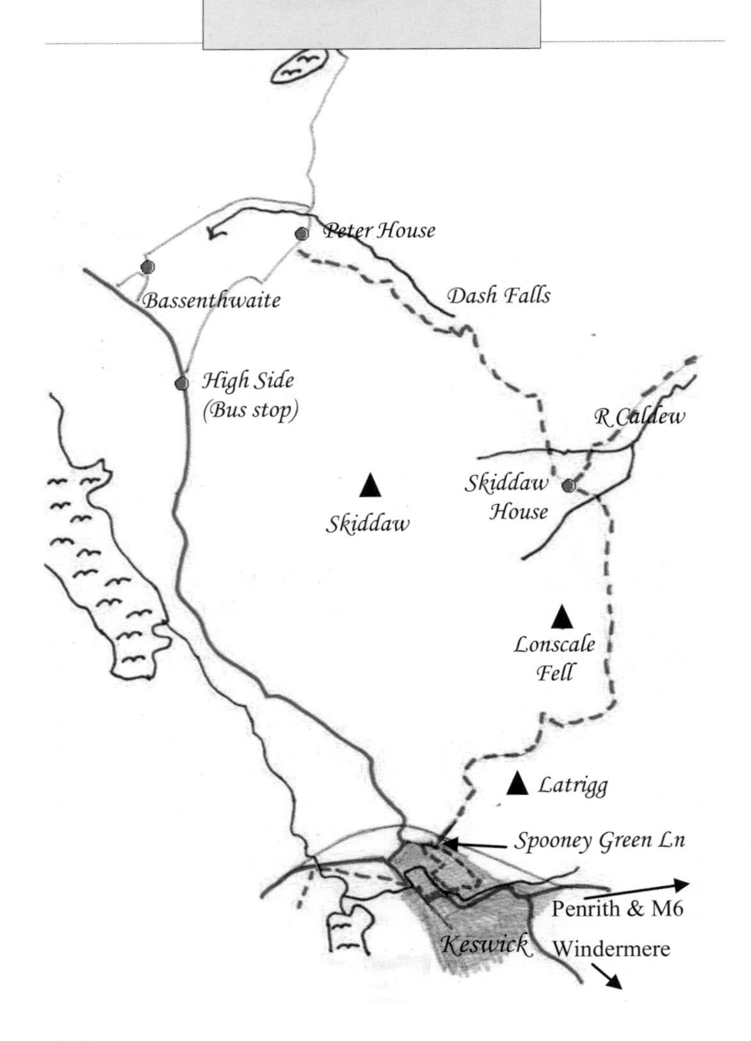

CUMBRIA WAY
SECTION 4 (North)
Skiddaw House to Caldbeck
E route via High Pike
15km (9½ miles)
W route via Orthwaite
20km (12½ miles)

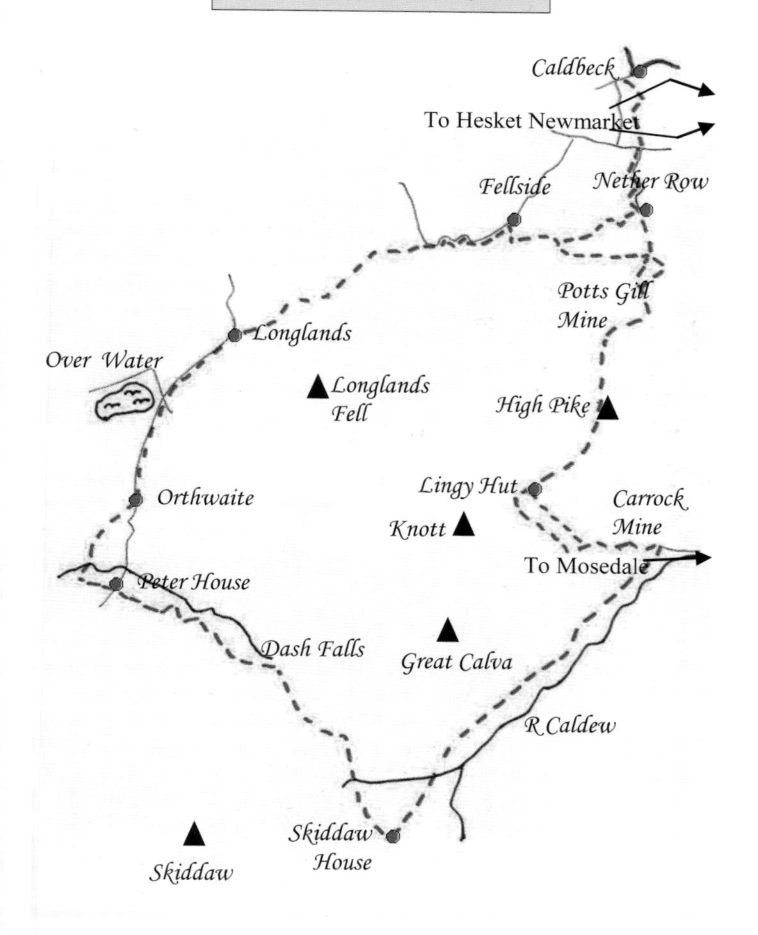

Place	Walk summary
Keswick	
Skiddaw House	9km from Keswick: upland walking on good paths.
Main route:	
(Mosedale)	5.6km gradual descent on broad path from Skiddaw House to Carrock Mine. Mosedale is 3km off route E on small road. *NB Café not open all the time and bus is infrequent.*
Lingy Hut	2.3km from Carrock Mine. A choice of routes, the unofficial alternative having a clearer path than the official route–see route notes for details. Almost no facilities at the hut other than a roof over your head.
Caldbeck	Main route: 9.5km fell walk over High Pike from Carrock Mine. Paths sometimes very sketchy on hig ground.
(Hesket Newmarket)	2km SE off route SE of Caldbeck but can be reache direct from High Pike area and Nether Row.
Alternative route:	
Peter House	5.7km easy descent on landrover track from Skidda House on W (alternative) route. Bus is 2km off rout down road (at High Side).
(Bassenthwaite)	400m across field from Peter House to junction wit Bassenthwaite FP. Village is 1.6km off route on descending FP across fields. *NB 73 bus to Caldbeck very infrequent.*
Caldbeck	Field paths and quiet roads almost 15km from Peter House. Lots of (mostly small) ups and downs.
(Hesket Newmarket)	2km SE off route SE of Caldbeck. Can be reached direct from Nether Row.

CTION 4 OF THE CUMBRIA WAY

el	B&B etc.	YH/ Barn	Camp-site	Café Pub	Shop	PO	Bank	ATM	Tel box	Bus/ Boat	Train
	✓	✓	✓	✓	✓	✓	✓	✓	✓	lots boat	
		✓									
	✓			✓					✓	73	
	✓		✓	✓	✓	✓		✓	✓	73 74	
	✓	✓		✓						73	
										73 554 X58	
	✓		✓	✓					✓	73 554 X58	
	✓		✓	✓	✓	✓		✓	✓	73 74	
	✓	✓		✓						73	

4.1
700m

WP 083 Moot Hall, Keswick

Apart from Ulverston and Carlisle, Keswick is the biggest place on the Cumbria Way. If you have any stocking up to do, do it here. Caldbeck is a good day's walk away and, although it has a couple of shops, you won't get the range of stuff that you will in Keswick. There are no refreshments to be had actually on the route between Keswick and Caldbeck so make sure that you set off with enough to keep you going!

There are various ways out of Keswick to pick up the CW. The official route (on OS maps) goes via the old railway station and Brundholme Road, and there are some guidebooks that suggest you go via High Hill and the main A591. The author's preferred option follows the official route into Station Street and as far as the Youth Hostel, but then turns off to cross Fitz Park, a super place to walk even in pouring rain! It's up to you, of course, but so long as we all meet up again at the bottom of Spooney Green Lane–see the street maps at the end of Section 3–it'll all be OK. (These notes start from the Moot Hall and take the Fitz Park option.)

Head south-east from the Moot Hall (with Lloyds TSB on your L) and in 50m turn left at the pub into Station Street. Follow this to the main road which you cross and then continue ahead onto Station Road. In 250m, just after passing the entrance to the YHA and crossing the bridge over the River Greta, turn left into Fitz Park. Walk down the tarmac path alongside the river with the playing fields etc. on your right. In 350m come to a junction of paths.
(WP 084) (E 326591 N 523841 (NY 265238)).

4.2
550m

WP 084 Turn R at this junction in Fitz Park

There are a few photos now taken in the pouring rain: the author would hate you to think the sun always shines on guide-book writers!

Turn right and then, after passing a stone barn-like building with a slate roof, turn left. The path runs alongside trees and emerges onto a road where you turn right. Walk gently uphill past a few houses (Briar Rigg) and look out for Spooney Green Lane which is sign-posted on your left.
(WP 085) (E 326766 N 524108 (NY 267241)).

4.3
2.2km

WP 085 The start of Spooney Green Lane. The cloud-covered hill is Latrigg

4.3 cont Turn left (or right if you have come from the old railway station direction) into Spooney Green Lane.

Walk up this broad track which soon crosses the Keswick by-pass (by a bridge thankfully) and then reaches and passes the house of Spooney Green (*B&B*).

For the next 2km or so it is just a matter of following the obvious track as it climbs–quite steeply at first–up to a parking area at Gale Road. Avoid turning off left or right, staying with the main track at all times. There is just one place where there may be a little doubt and that is where there appears to be a choice of routes. This occurs fairly early in the climb and is not far after a path joins yours from the right and the route makes a sharp left-hand bend as it crosses a little stream. The easiest way to describe it is to carry straight on at the first apparent choice, follow the path round sharp right and then go left at the crossroads of paths.

Go straight ahead and follow the path round to the right...

...and then turn left at this crossroads of paths

It's all very straightforward if you remember that your path is climbing across the flank of the hillside, so that you always have ground rising to your right and falling to your left. The gradient eases and there is plenty of opportunity to admire the views back over Keswick and Derwentwater.

Eventually, after passing Gale Ghyll Woods on your left and a path signposted for "Latrigg Summit", our route steepens again briefly to bring you to the Gale Road car park. Turn right to walk to the end of the parking area.
(WP 086) (E 328079 N 525331 (NY 280253)).

4.4 350m	Go through the gate/stile and turn left onto a clear path running alongside the wall and fence.

In 350m, you come to an obvious fork at a set of gates.
(WP 087) (E 328288 N 525563 (NY 282255)).

4.5 4.4km

WP 087 Take the right hand fork here NOT the left one heading uphill

Take the right-hand fork (CW waymark on gate). (The left fork, even in weather as murky as it was when the photo was taken, is clearly heading uphill: it is the most commonly used route for the walk up to the summit of Skiddaw.) The good, broad path you're on descends slightly and turns sharp right as it crosses Whit Beck. This is a great place to stop for a brew on the right sort of day so, once you're suitably refreshed, carry on with the excellent path as it rises gently around the south-eastern shoulder of Lonscale Fell. Just keep an eye and an ear out for cyclists hurtling down towards you.

1200m (about 15-20 mins) from Whit Beck, you go through a gate/ stile. Almost immediately the character of the path changes. You're now high above the steep-sided valley of the River Glenderaterra and the path, although still broad, becomes, just briefly, very rocky underfoot. Nervous walkers may feel a little intimidated by the drop, but the path is fine and is used by loads of walkers and cyclists. In rain and ice the rocks may be slippery. If you don't like the drop stay well to the left and you should have no difficulties. This rocky section lasts only for a minute or two, after which the path pulls itself together and starts to behave impeccably again.

4.5 cont

The views into and across the Glenderaterra valley to the great grassy wall of Blencathra are, needless to say, very impressive.

The rocky section on the path above the Glenderaterra valley

Just keep on keeping on, hopefully with the weather being kind enough to allow you to enjoy the views. Even in poor weather, though, this is all great: an unmissable path with no navigation problems and an enormous sense of being really amongst the hills. The path splashes across a couple of small streams coming down the hillside to your left and then makes a short stony descent, near the bottom of which a small path branches off right. Ignore this, staying with the main path which soon crosses a bigger stream at a footbridge. The path rises again past a ruined building and then a flat-topped boulder (marked as Guide Stone on the OS map) at a path junction. Again ignore the path branching off and keep ahead soon being joined by a wall on your right. This keeps you company for 400m or so before it bends away right and, in a further 350m, just after the path loses itself a little in wetter ground, arrive at a gate where the view over the wild Skiddaw Forest opens out ahead of you. (This is forest in its old sense of "unenclosed land used for hunting": apart from a bedraggled plantation around Skiddaw House, you will struggle to see many trees around here.)
(WP 088) (E 329374 N 528781 (NY 293287)).

4.6 800m	Keep ahead through the gate and follow the path as it bends left towards the lonely building of Skiddaw House, set in its surround of straggly conifers.

Cross the footbridge over the cheerful stream of Salehow Beck and climb up to Skiddaw House (*YHA*). Walk alongside the wall in front of the building and, at its end, arrive at a waymark post.
(WP 089) (E 328725 N 529148 (NY 287291)).

Approaching Skiddaw House

This waymark post, just at the end of the "garden wall" of Skiddaw House, is a significant point on the journey.

It is here that you have to decide, if you haven't already, whether you're going for the higher-level, eastern alternative over High Pike, or the so-called low-level western alternative via Orthwaite and Longlands. There is no space in this part of the notes to go into details about the merits and demerits of each. For what it's worth, in the author's opinion, the High Pike route is ***much*** *better even though, in cloud, navigation to the top of High Pike may not be entirely straightforward. But then, you do have these notes!*

It might be a heresy to suggest this, but you could always take the High Pike route as far as Carrock Mine before making your decision. If, by then, you don't like the look of the walk up to High Pike, you could go down the delightful road to Mosedale, there turning left to follow a very scenic road below Carrock Fell to Calebreck Farm. From there, either fashion a route across country to Nether Row, or stick with the road to Hesket Newmarket and then Caldbeck. It is about the same distance as the official western route. And, as at 2011, between 11 April and 30 October, there is a bus from Mosedale to Caldbeck (18.43 every day, and on Saturday, there's one at 15.01 as well). And probably no angry buzzard to deal with either. Just a thought...

The notes continue with the eastern alternative (i.e. the route via the summit of High Pike) as this is the option that appears to be by far the more frequently used. The western option (via Orthwaite and Longlands) starts at paragraph 4.19.

4.7
5.6km

Eastern (Higher Level) Route via Grainsgill Beck, Lingy Hut and High Pike.

Turn right at the waymark post and follow the grassy path gently downhill alongside a wall.

The start of the main (eastern) route from Skiddaw House

For the next 5.6km (3½ miles), all the way to the tarmac road at the foot of Grainsgill Beck, it is simply a matter of following the clear path as it trundles along the eastern base of, first Great Calva, and then, Knott. This is very easy walking–almost as easy as anything on the CW–and you can bowl along with no navigational worries at all. But the way is long and the scenery changes very little. Most walkers will take at least an hour and a quarter from Skiddaw House–probably more–to reach Grainsgill Beck, so don't expect this bit to end too soon. The wide open spaces are great though. Detailed directions aren't necessary but just a few highlights are mentioned so that you can tick them off as you go.

About 500m from Skiddaw House the path swings sharp left and then right to cross the River Caldew at a substantial footbridge.

Then, after a brief climb away from the Caldew, the path resumes its downward course and 800m after the footbridge passes a circular sheepfold. A further 800m brings you to another circular sheepfold immediately followed by a footbridge (over Wiley Gill) and a gate and stile.

Circular sheepfold, footbridge and gate/stile at Wiley Gill

750m later, the path passes what looks like a rectangular sheepfold, this one with a ruined building nearby, and 700m further on, after passing a lone pine tree, you ford the stream of Burdell Gill.

4.7 cont

After Burdell Gill, the path becomes vehicle width and appears to divide.

Don't take the left branch heading uphill, but keep to the right-hand (main) path which stays fairly level and parallel to the river which, here, is 40–50m away. Just follow the broad easy track as it stays fairly close to the river and in 1.8km from Burdell Gill (about 25 minutes) passes a parking area down to the right and crosses a substantial bridge over Grainsgill Beck
(WP 090) (E 332676 N 532696 (NY 326326)).

4.8 500m

WP 090 Looking up Grainsgill Beck from the bridge. The Lingy Hut can be seen on the skyline

This is the last chance to change your mind about walking over High Pike. If you really can't face the climb–although by the time you reach Lingy Hut, you'll have done just about all the hard work–or the weather is poor and you're not confident in your navigational skills and/or with these notes, then you will have to turn right and walk down the road to the hamlet of Mosedale 3km away. (Phone box (no coins), a couple of B&Bs, tearoom (open till 5pm in summer) and a summer bus service to Hesket Newmarket and Caldbeck– ***check timetables before leaving Keswick!)*** *From Mosedale you can walk to Hesket Newmarket and Caldbeck on the road–very pleasant in parts because of open grassland to walk on if you prefer. From Calebreck, there is a not totally straightforward public footpath which rejoins the official route at Nether Row, or you can stay on the road all the way–but it's narrow and, after Howbeck, quite busy, so is not ideal.*

Assuming you're carrying on with the High Pike option, the official way turns right off the bridge, follows the tarmac road for less than 50m and then turns sharp left up a semi-surfaced mine road at a metal barrier with a waymarked signpost. Or, you could save yourself a bit of walking by using a rough short cut opposite the bridge for a few metres and then turning left onto the mine road.

Either way, follow the mine road gently uphill to pass in 500m a notice about mineral collection. You will now be in an area of old mine tips where vegetation is struggling to regain any kind of roothold. The abandoned mine buildings on the opposite side of the stream are clearly in view and the track comes to a fork.
(WP 091) (E 332288 N 532941 (NY 322329)).

4.9
130m

WP 091 The first fork at Carrock Mine–keep right (uphill)

Keep right and take the uphill branch (a green track). In 130m this swings sharp right. Do not follow it but instead leave it by keeping straight ahead, slightly uphill, on a sketchy path across a stony patch of grassy ground. *(Photo on next page.)* In just a dozen or so paces, arrive at a sort of crossroads where a clear green track follows a level course off to the left. There was a small marker cairn here in September 2011, but it looked a bit frail so might not last long.
(WP 092) (E 332168 N 533004 (NY 321330)).

An unofficial route to Lingy Hut goes straight ahead here and is described in paragraph 4.13. The official route (as shown on the map) goes left along that level track and is described first (paragraphs 4.10 to 4.12).

Both routes are OK but, in the author's opinion, the official route— which stays alongside the stream for most of the way to the skyline—has become too badly eroded to be really enjoyable, especially in or after wet weather. The unofficial variant is, after the first few paces, on a clearer path and, for most of its length, on firmer ground. For these reasons, the author recommends the variant as described in paragraph 4.13.

NB It should perhaps go without saying that old mine workings can be dangerous. There are no problems with either of the routes described in these notes but if you wander off the path and come to any old workings, stay well away from them!

4.10
450m

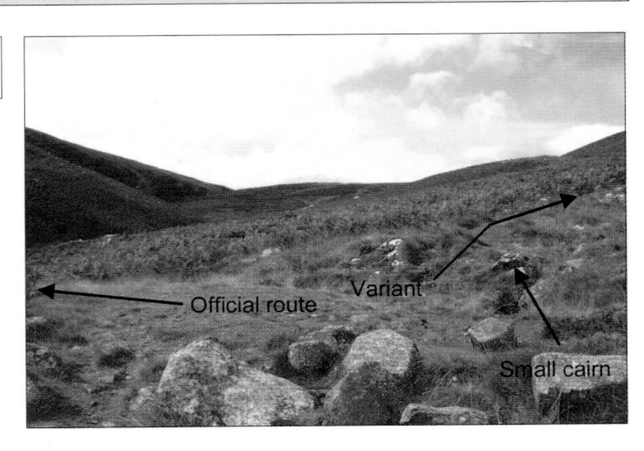

For the official route, go left along the broad level track. For the poor-weather variant, go straight ahead on the smaller path uphill

For the official route, go left on the almost level green path which leads easily to the bank of the stream and, from here, it is really just a case of picking your way along the narrow, but generally easy to follow, path that is muddy in places, rocky in others, but always a joy to walk–when the weather's kind, that is.

The path stays mostly down by the water's edge, moving away onto the bank tops only when the stream sides close in and become steeper. It is certainly worth watching for the frequent changes of direction that the path makes as it seeks out the easiest and most comfortable way up the valley: there is no need to be floundering about in deep heather, that's for sure. In 450m (about 10-15 minutes allowing for the climbing), you reach a side stream, the unusually named Arm o'Grain.
(WP 093) (E 331740 N 533092 (NY 317330)).

4.11
850m

WP 093 Crossing Arm o'Grain on the official route

Cross the stream–usually easy just above the tree in the photo, but you may have to make a longish detour upstream in wet conditions: *if this is the case, you could join the variation route which crosses Arm o'Grain at some ruined buildings 100m or so upstream*. Otherwise, keep ahead in similar style, passing a couple of small waterfalls before coming to a longer one straight ahead. Here the path starts to move a little bit away (right) from the streamside and it becomes a little indefinite but remains visible. (It stays roughly parallel to the stream and is never more than about 30m away from it.) It passes through a bouldery section and comes to a much larger flat-topped boulder (almost the size of a small car). About 30m after the boulder is a vague fork. It doesn't much matter which branch you take although the left-hand one is probably easier to navigate by in poor weather. This left branch comes alongside the stream again more or less exactly at the point where you have to change direction.
(WP 094) (E 331000 N 533235 (NY 310332)).

In good weather, there will be no problems here (apart from wet feet, maybe) because the Lingy Hut is now clearly visible 350m away to the right. In mist and rain, this will be a fairly uninspiring sort of a spot–for most people at any rate. There are no precipices to fall over, but you don't want to be wandering around like lost souls up here, do you? (This is another reason why the variation route (see para 4.13) is recommended in less than ideal conditions.) It is worth keeping a sharp eye out for the path that links the Great Lingy Hut with the summit of Knott. So far, you should have been walking on some kind of path, however small; once past the cross-path that you need there are no paths–just the marshland of Miller Moss. The cross path you want arrives just where the slope changes from steady to almost imperceptible. If you find yourself heading west across pathless, nearly flat land which, almost certainly will be wet underfoot, you've probably gone too far, and will need to turn right to head north-east.

4.12
400m

At the junction turn right (north-north-east) onto the Knott– High Pike path.

This very soon becomes much wider and clearer and quickly arrives at the Lingy Hut–unmistakeable: it's the only building for miles. **(WP 095)** (E 331173 N 533578 (NY 311335)).
Go to paragraph 4.14.

The back end of the Lingy Hut–complete with CW waymark!

4.13
1.2km

For the unofficial variation route to Lingy Hut from Carrock Mine (WP 092), go straight ahead uphill on an initially somewhat sketchy path which very soon becomes much clearer as it develops into a grassy way through bracken.

The gradient eases and the almost level walking is a delight. In 500m (from the start of the variation route at the small cairn) cross the stream of Arm o'Grain (usually easy) to come to some (very) ruined buildings. The path now swings right to run more or less parallel to the stream. Although not (yet) beaten out into a firm path, the way should not be in doubt. After a wettish patch, the path begins the main part of the ascent to Lingy Hut as it climbs a grassy bank, where a line of footprints serves as an excellent guide. Watch out for the point where the path bends left away from the stream to climb a little more steeply. The place is about 200m from where you crossed the stream and the way ahead is up a dark line with obvious foot marks: the direction is north-west. Gradually, the steepness eases and the path becomes a clear line on grass. As the path passes an isolated large boulder, Lingy Hut appears ahead (weather permitting), and is soon reached up a simple grassy slope. You rejoin the main route by turning right onto the good path that passes the hut. **(WP 095)** (E 331173 N 533578 (NY 311335)).

Lingy Hut has been recently repaired, and is maintained by the LDNPA and a notice inside says that it is used as a rest and sleeping point by over 1000 people on the CW each year. Good folk, such as the users of this guide, will obviously ensure that they leave the hut at least as tidy as they found it.

Looking back to the Lingy Hut and Blencathra

4.14 1.3km

Keep ahead from the hut on the obvious broad track, soon passing right of a rectangular sheepfold 35m or so from the track.

The track rises gently almost to the very summit of the grassy hill of Hare Stones and High Pike comes into view, not very far away, but clearly higher.

High Pike from the broad track over Hare Stones

In clear weather you'll be able to see two converging paths heading for the summit of High Pike: they show up as dark lines in the grass. It doesn't matter which one you use but, in misty conditions, the second one will be easier to find. The track over Hare Stones is now wide and stony and descends slightly as it bends to the right. About 250m after the bend the track–almost level–comes to a junction with a smaller path coming in from Carrock Fell to your right.
(WP 096) (E 331864 N 534630 (NY 318346)).

4.15 450m

Turn left here onto a much smaller path which, however, remains easy to follow all the way up easy grassy slopes to the summit of High Pike.
(WP 097) (E 331875 N 535010 (NY 318350)).

The summit of High Pike (658m or 2157 ft).
The highest point on the CW and the only fell in the Lake District with a slate seat on the top. Terrific, eh?

The top of High Pike is in no sense a pointy peak, but it is the most northerly of Lakeland's 2000ft summits and the view, when the weather permits, is vast. The Solway Firth and some of the Scottish Hills can be seen to the north and west, the Pennines march along the eastern horizon, and through the gap between Skiddaw and Blencathra to the south, you should get a view of old friends such as Bowfell and Crinkle Crags, now nearly 20 miles (30 km) distant. Apart from the summit cairn and the seat, there is a trig point on the top now adorned with a view indicator and, a little further away, the ruins of a shepherd's hut.

4.16
1.3km

The descent off High Pike is one of the gentlest in Lakeland but you do need to get the direction right.

Less than 100m from the trig point on the northern rim of the summit plateau is a small cairn and, a little further right, a larger heap of stones (all that remains of a shepherd's hut). From the trig point, head towards the ruined hut (due north) and then aim a little further west towards the twin TV masts. (If you can't see the masts, head due north off the top, keep to that bearing and all will be fine.)

4.16 cont	*Resist the temptation to use an improving path that heads off north-east from the area of the ruined hut: it will bring you back onto the broad stony track you left earlier and you could end up walking towards Hesket Newmarket–or even Mosedale–and not Caldbeck.*

Assuming you're aiming for those twin masts, you should, very soon after leaving the summit plateau, come upon one of two roughly parallel paths heading down the grassy hillside. If you can see them both, the right hand one is slightly better, but it doesn't matter a lot. So long as you're heading due north, or just slightly west of due north, it's fine. (*The line on the OS map runs slightly east of north which is also OK, but there's a danger that if you head just a bit too far east, you will miss the path leading you down through the abandoned Potts Gill mine area.*) In anything like decent weather you will be able to see Caldbeck almost directly ahead.

800m from the top (between 10 and 15 minutes for most walkers), you will meet a clearer path crossing the fell. Turn right along it and it soon swings left around the head of the valley of Potts Gill to bring you to a junction, which needs to be watched for.
(WP 098) (E 332101 N 536130 (NY 321361)).

4.17 500m	Turn left onto the clearer path and descend easily for 500m to reach an obvious crossroads of paths. (There are old mine tips and other evidence of defunct industrial activity around here, and there is more to come.) **(WP 099)** (E 332024 N 536626 (NY 320366)).

4.18
1.6km

Keep straight ahead to continue the easy descent. The old mine road (and the route of the CW) make a wide loop to the right (to reduce the gradient) but you can cut the corner if you wish by using a path that leaves the official way at a grass-covered pile of stones (about 300m or so from the crossroads).

Both options reunite at a wall corner *(along with an alternative route from Little Fellside Farm on the western route from Skiddaw House (para 4.29))* and then descend to go through a waymarked gate. Walk along the stony track and in about 150m arrive at a set of three gates in front of you (with a fourth gate a little further to the left). Take the middle gate of the three (new WMA) and walk on in front of the white building of Clay Bottom Farm.

Clay Bottom Farm

Leave the farm via the obvious track and in 200m arrive at a sort of triangular junction/parking area at the start of a tarmac road. This is Nether Row and is the place where the western (Orthwaite) option and your route re-join.
(WP 100) (E 332372 N 537807 (NY 323378)).

To continue with the route notes to Caldbeck, please go to Paragraph 4.30.

The notes now continue with the western alternative from Skiddaw House. The combined route from Nether Row to Caldbeck restarts at paragraph 4.30.

4.19 5.7km	**Western Alternative Route from Skiddaw House via Dash Falls, Orthwaite and Longlands.**

Bear slightly left at the Skiddaw House WMP (WP 089) to climb gently on grass and, in just a few paces, turn right on to the obvious land-rover track heading away north-westwards. Even in bad weather, this track is easy to follow. It descends for the first 500m or so to cross the headwaters of the River Caldew–usually fordable but there is a footbridge just in case you experience the same kind of weather the author did when he took this photo.

The ford and footbridge across the River Caldew in very wet weather

The track now climbs gently, bends left and crosses Dead Beck to reach the highest point of the day at about 490m. Now descending gently, the track remains easy to follow as it makes a left-right zig-zag to cross a stone bridge over Dash Beck and arrives at a gate and stile with views ahead over the farmland around Bassenthwaite. The descent steepens a little as the track winds down past the waterfalls of Whitewater Dash (Dash Falls).

The upside of walking in wet weather!
The top fall of Whitewater Dash.
If you want to get close to the falls for a look, TAKE EXTREME CARE!!

The broken cliffs up to your left are Dead Crags, a part of Skiddaw, and the track gets easier and easier until it joins the tarmac access road to Dash Farm. Bear left and follow this road down for a further 1.3km (15–20 mins) to come to the quiet Keswick–Orthwaite road near Peter House Farm.
(WP 101) (E 324918 N 532323 (NY 249323)).

Before you go any further, there is a decision to be made. If you're heading back to Keswick for another night's B&B there and you need to catch a bus, you will have to get to the main road A591: either turn left at Peter House and follow the small road to where it joins the main road at High Side (about 2km), or walk across fields to Bassenthwaite village and then use the road to the main road at the chapel (Buses do not serve Bassenthwaite village centre). The Bassenthwaite option has the advantage of taking you to a village with a pub–the Sun Inn–but it does involve a little bit of route finding.

4.20
350m

Assuming you're going for the official route, take the stile/gate at WP 101 and head across the open field, aiming slightly further right than the signpost (for Bassenthwaite and Orthwaite) is pointing. (But don't take the farm track that leads away from the gate)

You need to head for the right-hand end of the plantation. As you approach it, a path develops and this takes you to a gate near an electricity pole. Go through and come to a four-way signpost.
(WP 102) (E 324604 N 532447 (NY 246324)).
(*Go straight on here if you're heading to Bassenthwaite.*)

4.21
750m

WP 102. Go through the gate to come to the 4-way signpost, and turn R for the CW (straight on for Bassenthwaite)

Turn right at the SP (CW; Orthwaite) and walk alongside the conifer hedge. Continue ahead passing through a couple of gates to enter a field with the buildings of Kestrel Lodge to your left. Keep on in the same line parallel to the right hand field boundary to cross a tree-lined stream in a dip and go through another gate (or over the stile) into a field that had just been reseeded in July 2011. Walk alongside the right hand field boundary (watch out for the barbed wire) and, in 150m or so, at the end of the field, turn right through an unwaymarked gate into a rougher field at the top of a slope. Either go directly down the slope or, easier on the old joints, head diagonally downhill away from the gate to join a track where you may or may not see a waymark post. Turn sharp left onto the track and follow it down through a gate to a footbridge in woodland.
(WP 103) (E 324466 N 533113 (NY 244331)).

WP 103. Cross the footbridge and head up to the road

4.22
250m

Cross the bridge and turn right to walk along the forest track to arrive, after only 50m, at a narrow tarmac road.

(You can turn right here and follow the road for 700m to its junction with the Orthwaite road. Turning left there would bring you in 1100m to Orthwaite to rejoin the official route at paragraph 4.24.)

To continue with the official route go straight across the road and climb steeply through the trees (SP) just above a stream down to your right. After a few minutes the climb eases a little and the path swings left away from the stream to head towards a corrugated iron hut with a large flat-topped boulder in front of it. Before reaching these objects the path bends away right and soon brings you to a waymarked stile next to a gate.
(WP 104) (E 324414 N 533324 (NY 244333)).

4.23
950m

Cross the stile and go ahead for a few steps to bear right onto a stony cart track which swings further right to cross the stream.

Arrive at a new gate and stile (with no waymarks as at July 2011). (*The route on the OS map goes straight on here along a clear track but this is not marked as a right of way. The route described in these notes is the "traditional" way following the right of way heading north-east and passing just left of the 237m spot height on the map.*) Once through the gate/stile, leave the good track and head across pathless grass aiming just left of the highest point of the field.

Go through/ over the un-waymarked gate/stile onto the good track, but leave it almost immediately to walk across grass aiming just left of the summit of the field

As this small hill is crested you should be able to pick out a ladder stile in the far (north-east) corner of the field. Walk down to cross that stile (SPs) and continue ahead in roughly the same direction, aiming just right of the top of the small gorse-covered hill in front. Walk through the gorse on a narrow path just below the summit with a good view down to your right of Little Tarn.

You are now entering the Buzzard's Domain, so do stay alert! As you cross the hill, you should be able to spot a broad wooden bridge spanning the stream that flows out of the northern end of Little Tarn. Head down the grassy bank to cross the bridge, passing over some wetter ground on the way. Almost immediately over the bridge come to a stile in the fence on the left.
(WP 105) (E 324886 N 533974 (NY 248339)).

WP 105. Cross the stile and head up the field to a gate and stile just left of the biggest tree in the photo

4.24 400m	Cross the stile and maintain the NE direction you have been walking in, heading up the field towards the biggest tree in the photo.

Just left of that tree, go through/cross another gate/stile. (This is the epicentre of any buzzard activity.) Walk up the gently rising field alongside the right-hand field boundary (fence and trees) for just over 150m, ignoring on the way a metal gate giving onto a cart track. At the end of the field, cross a stile next to a gate and head straight across the field following the line in the grass, aiming for the right-hand end of the largeish house. Cross a stone stile to reach the road where this route and the road route from Peter House reunite.
(WP 106) (E 325247 N 534094 (NY 252340)).

4.25
2.3km

Turn left onto the road and follow it for a little over 2km (about half an hour or so).

The road is quiet and pleasant and there are no navigation problems–just keep straight ahead at the only junction you come to. The main items of interest are the pink house of Orthwaite Hall and the lakes of Over Water and Chapelhouse Reservoir. Just after the reservoir the road makes a fairly steep climb up to Lowthwaite and then descends to cross Longlands Beck at a bend. Immediately after the bend and just before the houses of Longlands is a signposted gate on the right.
(WP 107) (E 326619 N 535877 (NY 266358)).

4.26
2.7km

Go through the gate onto an excellent track heading left. This first passes behind the gardens of the houses in Longlands and then runs alongside a plantation enclosed by a well-made stone wall.

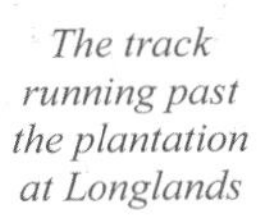

The track running past the plantation at Longlands

The track then moves away from the plantation and continues to climb gently and, as it nears the top of its climb, you should, in clear weather, get a view left of the Solway Firth. The track swings right revealing a massive view ahead of rolling farmland with the Pennines in the far distance. Clearly you are at the northern edge now of the Lakeland fells so enjoy this fine, airy walking. As the track levels ignore a path branching off right for Great Sca Fell. A short descent leads to the ford at Charleton Wath where there is a new plantation of mixed native trees. The track becomes stonier now and is joined by a wall on the left.

A long, gradual descent brings you down to join the tarmac access road from Rough Close. Keep ahead, still descending gently, and pass Howburn (marked as Holborn on some maps) Farm. Soon arrive at a junction with a slightly bigger road at Green Head.
(WP 108) (E 328618 N 537062 (NY 286370)).

4.27 2.1km

Turn right and follow the road–once again, quiet and relatively traffic free.

Cross the stone bridge over the wonderfully-named Burblethwaite Beck and on past Askew Mire Farm and so through the picturesque hamlet of Branthwaite.

Branthwaite

Keep ahead on the road which climbs steeply out of Branthwaite to pass the former school. There is a handily placed bench to sit on near the top of the steep bit and just after this the road enters the hamlet of Fell Side. *(NB the phone box marked on some maps is no longer there.)* The road continues to climb–but very gently now–as you walk all the way through Fell Side to pass the last building on the right–an impressive house that is now used as an outdoor education centre. Immediately after the end of the tall stone wall of this building is a lane going off to the right (CW waymark on the opposite side of the road).
(WP 109) (E 330544 N 537597 (NY 330375)).
If you've had enough, Caldbeck can be reached by staying on the road; it's not much closer that way, but it might be a bit easier.

4.28
800m

To stay with the route of the CW, turn right up the lane to go in 120m through a gate onto a concrete road with a grassy middle.

This climbs a little as it swings left and soon brings you to the entrance to Little Fellside Farm. The concrete track drops down left through the gate but the CW goes on ahead onto grass, where there is a WMP.
(WP 110) (E 331209 N 537301 (NY 312373)).

4.29
1.7km

WP 110
At Little
Fellside Farm

You have a choice here: the route as it appears on the map (more or less) is described first, and is the shortest way to Nether Row, where both alternatives meet up. The other way is, in the author's opinion, incomparably better, and appears to be the way the CW waymark arrows are pointing.

For the route on the map, do not enter the farm but keep ahead on grass staying alongside the garden wall. Walk past another gate (that leads into the farm area), after which the path becomes briefly clearer on the ground as it veers right to move away from the wall a little. The path then encounters an area of wetter ground with tall rushes and just about disappears, but you can see your next objective, Potts Gill Farm, just ahead. Make use of whatever bits of path you can find to walk parallel to the wall/fence on your left and about 30m or so away from it. Cross a stream as the farm is approached and then head left (downhill) aiming for a small gate at the right-hand end of the buildings and garden.

The way into Potts Gill Farm

Go through this gate and then follow a succession of WMAs down to the farm access road. Turn right past a big corrugated iron barn and follow the access road/lane easily for 800m or so to arrive at the triangle of roads at Nether Row.
(WP 111) (E 332366 N 537811 (NY 323378)).

This is where the eastern and western alternative routes from Skiddaw House rejoin. Go to paragraph 4.30.

For the alternative (better) route from Little Fellside (WP 110), walk past the WMP for a dozen or so paces and then, just before reaching the electricity pole, take a grassy track slanting gently uphill to the right between rushes. Although a little wet in places the path is very good–certainly better than the wet slog through the rushes lower down–and is reminiscent of the walk around Longlands Fell. The very slight climb levels out as the path follows the line between rushes (left) and bracken (on the steeper hillside above you). About 600m from Little Fellside the path crosses the stream of Potts Gill and climbs a little to come to a wall corner. A CW waymark points you left downhill here to Potts Gill Farm. If you take this option go down to the farm and through the small gate mentioned above. But it is much better to carry on along your good track, now with a wall to your left. In 250m, where the wall bends left downhill, this excellent track joins the main CW coming down from High Pike.
(For directions from here to Nether Row please see Paragraph 4.18.)

4.30
1.3km

If you've arrived at Nether Row via Potts Gill Farm, turn left; otherwise continue straight ahead.

Either way, take the small tarmac road heading north from Nether Row towards Caldbeck. Ignore a public footpath going off right (FP route to Hesket Newmarket) and in about 1km (15 minutes or so) from Nether Row come to a crossroads (turn R for road to Hesket Newmarket). For Caldbeck, go straight across onto a very narrow lane and in 200m come to a gate on the right with a sign advising you that it is not the route of the CW which, it says, is 75 yards further down the lane. Keep on and in 40m come to a SP pointing right across grass. Follow its direction and very soon reach an almost hidden stile just left of a gate giving onto an overgrown lane.
(WP 112) (E 332243 N 539105 (NY 322391)).

WP 112

The stile almost hidden by wild flowers

Cross the stile into a very neat field and head diagonally left to go through a metal gate less than 50m away. Keep on in the same direction across this small field (which adjoins the back garden of the neighbouring house) aiming between a gate and an electricity pole. Leave the field by a stile onto a narrow lane, go straight across and enter the next field via a kissing gate next to another electricity pole. Walk down the field alongside the left-hand field boundary and when, after about 200m, this moves away left, keep straight ahead, passing just left of the electricity pole to reach a waymarked gate into woodland.
(WP 113) (E 332256 N 539495 (NY 322394)).

4.32
400m

WP 113 Where the field boundary moves away left, keep ahead passing just left of the electricity pole to reach the gate into woodland

Descend on a narrow but clear path and cross a stream at a hump-backed stone bridge. The path is broader now as it passes along a tunnel of greenery and then past a row of modern houses to come to the main road B5299. Turn right to reach a road junction at the Old Smithy (tea rooms and shop). Keep ahead for another few paces to reach the Oddfellows Arms.
(WP 114) (E 332413 N 539757 (NY 324397)).

Caldbeck

CALDBECK

www.openstreetmap.org

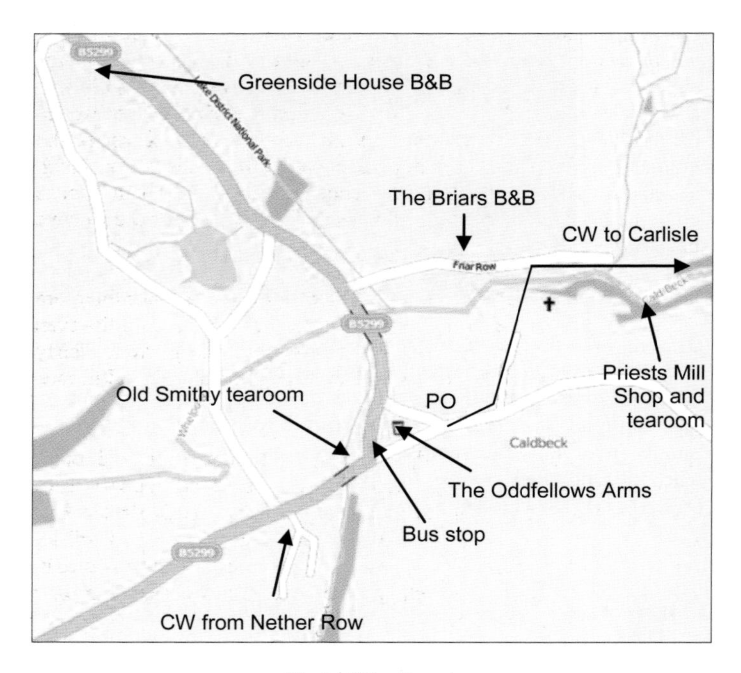

End of Section 4

SECTION 5: CALDBECK TO CARLISLE

24.5km (15 miles); 180m (600 ft) of ascent.

Apart from the first part–between Caldbeck and Sebergham Bridge–where there are some ups and downs and one or two rough and/or slippery paths, the rest of this Section is very gentle. Essentially it is a walk down the valley of the River Caldew (which you first met up on the hills near Skiddaw House), and, once past Sebergham, the gradients are as simple as they look on the Profile. This is very much a walk through gentle English countryside and the main hazard could be flooding in the riverside meadows–but it does need to have been pretty wet for that to happen.

Generally the scenery is pleasant rather than exciting, but there are frequent opportunities to look back towards the Lakeland hills–even from the old city walls in Carlisle. The easy gradients make for fairly rapid progress, but much of the riverside walking is too good to race through.

You will probably be used, by now, to refreshments and other facilities not being generally available on the CW and this applies to the first two-thirds of this Section too. Once you reach Bridge End there are options: there is a pub and there are buses to Carlisle; Dalston offers refreshments and buses (and trains) to Carlisle and, once Cummersdale is reached, you are never far from the main road (with buses) into Carlisle.

This Section has been described as a "winding-down" stage and, in some ways, it is. But navigation isn't always totally straightforward and the first part through the woods of Parson's Park can be muddy and time-consuming. It's also 15 miles long: don't underestimate it!

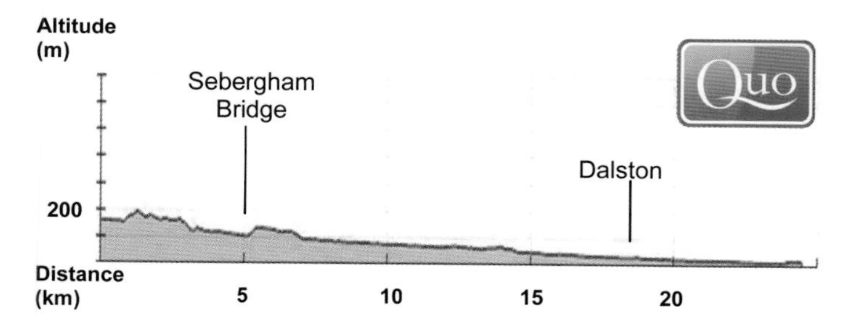

CUMBRIA WAY
SECTION 5 (South)
Caldbeck to Bridge End
14.5km (9 miles)

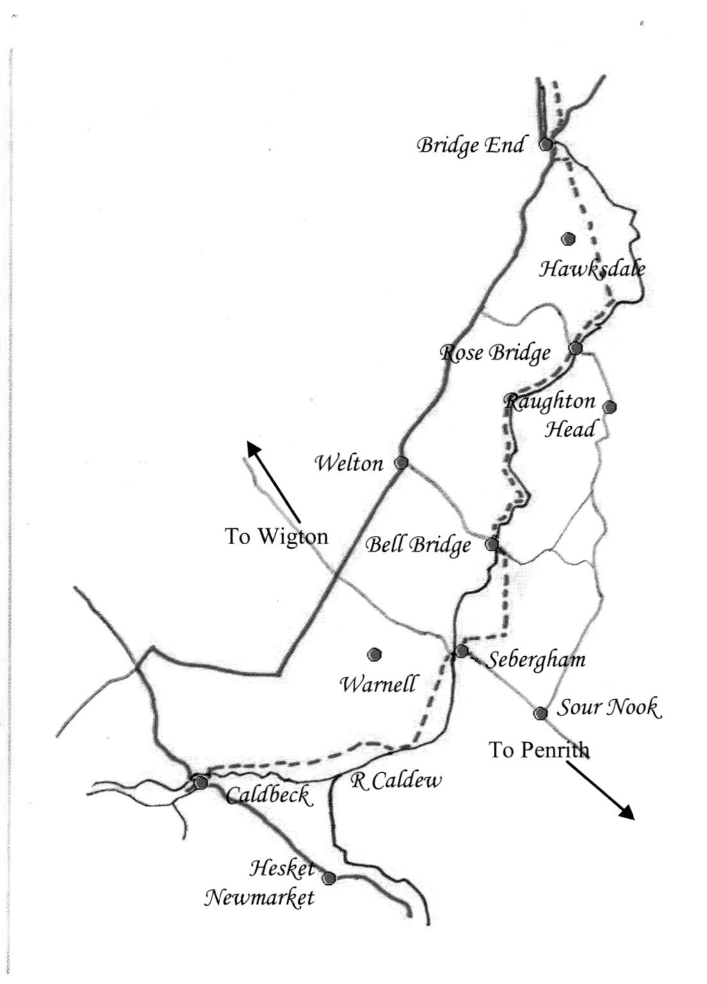

CUMBRIA WAY
SECTION 5 (North)
Bridge End to Carlisle
10km (6¼ miles)

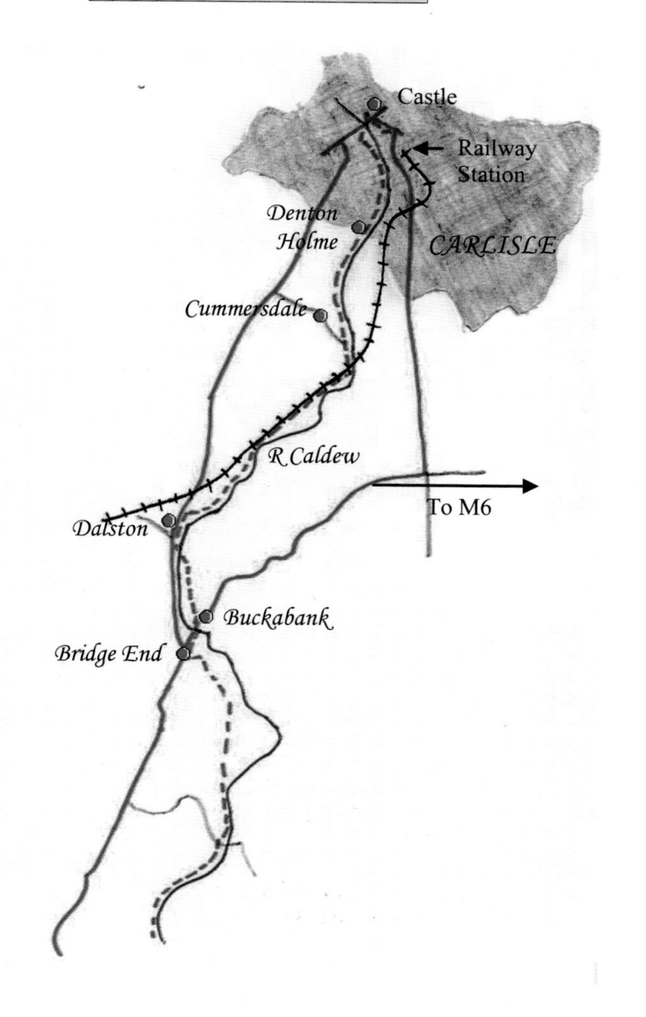

Place	Walk summary
Caldbeck	
(Hesket Newmarket)	*NB There is a FP going N from Hesket Newmarket to Parkhead. This runs alongside the R Caldew at first and then crosses Cald Beck via a FB before climbing up a field to join the CW part way through paragrap 5.5. (Or, if you want to do every step of the CW, you have to go back to Caldbeck.)*
(Warnell)	4.8km from Caldbeck on muddy woodland paths to path junction for Warnell. B&B 1km off route uphill. (See notes para 5.9).
Sebergham	5.2km from Caldbeck on mostly muddy woodland paths. Phone is 600m off route along main road and pub (Sour Nook) 1km further. B&B just off route near bridge. NB A "brew-your-own" hot drink service is sometim available in the vestry at Sebergham Church.
(Hawksdale Hall)	7.7km from Sebergham. First 2km broad tracks to Bell Bridge, then mostly riverside walking–easy but possible flooding problems. B&B just off route.
Bridge End	1.6km from Hawksdale Hall on field paths.
Dalston	1.6km from Bridge End all on level tarmac. Hotel is 1.5km NE of village off route.
(Cummersdale)	Road end for Cummersdale is 4km from Dalston on level tarmac cycleway. Village 700m off route uphill.
Carlisle	8.4km from Dalston–mostly tarmac, but some riversi walking on grass.

CTION 5 OF THE CUMBRIA WAY

l	B&B etc.	YH/ Barn	Camp-Site	Café Pub	Shop	PO	Bank	ATM	Tel box	Bus/ Boat	Train
	✓		✓	✓	✓	✓		✓	✓	73 74	
	✓	✓		✓						73	
	✓										
	✓			✓					✓		
	✓										
				✓					✓	65 73 75	
				✓	✓			✓	✓	73 75	✓
				✓					✓	65	
	✓	✓		✓	✓	✓	✓	✓	✓	lots	✓

5.1 350m

Head away east from the Oddfellows along Caldbeck's main street, soon passing the store/PO on your left.

In about 100m turn left up a narrow lane (or ginnel) (SP to Friar Row) so that you have the churchyard on your right. The churchyard contains the grave of the huntsman, John Peel, one of Lakeland's most famous characters.

St Kentigern's Church, Caldbeck

Go to the end of the ginnel and cross a little stone bridge to come to Friar Row. *(The Briars B&B is just to the left from here.)* Turn right (or go straight on if coming from the Briars) and, in less than 100m, come to a gate.
(WP 115) (E 332609 N 539939 (NY 326399)).

5.2 300m

Ignore the public footpath going left and go through the gate which is the first of several on this stretch that have waymark arrows but no mention of the CW.

Follow the broad track ahead for 200m and reach a set of gates marked "Keep Out". Go right and walk around the fenced area (a sewage works) to arrive at another gate with a waymark arrow and no mention of the CW. (Ignore the stile just up the hill from the gate.)
(WP 116) (E 332915 N 539969 (NY 329399)).

5.3 550m

Go through the gate onto a broad, recently resurfaced track in the woodland of Parson's Park.

In a little over 100m a narrow overgrown footpath goes off to the right. Ignore this and stay with the surfaced bridleway (waymark post) as it curves left and climbs–quite sharply at first. As the gradient eases the new surfacing comes to an end and, although still wide and easy to follow, the track becomes very muddy in places and there are obvious signs that horses pass this way. Come to, and pass, another waymark post directing you away from taking another narrow, very overgrown footpath on the right.
(WP 117) (E 333421 N 539993 (NY 334399)).

5.4 500m

Bear left with the bridleway, soon passing another waymark post where a path joins yours from the left.

After coming to the highest point of today's walk (about 190m) the path levels out. A short descent brings you to a place where a gap in the trees allows a good view over to Carrock Fell and High Pike–a welcome reminder that you are still close to the Lakes fells.

The view to Carrock Fell from a gap in the trees in Parson's Park

A couple of minutes after this, the path comes to a gate that leads out of the wood with, yet again, a waymark arrow but no mention of the CW.
(WP 118) (E 333922 N 539957 (NY 339399)).

5.5
500m

Once through the gate the route on the OS map appears to go through/above the gorse and shrubs that you can see just ahead of you but, judging from the line in the grass, most walkers and horse riders take an easier way that stays just below the gorse bushes etc. So we'll go with the majority and take this line.

Follow the darker line in the grass and stay right of the bushes

About 400m (five minutes or so) after the gate, a fence should come into view ahead of you with a gate at its lower (right-hand) end by a wood. Just where the bushes on your left come to an end head slightly left on grass away from the bit of a path you're on. As you crest the little brow ahead of you, another (smaller) gate comes into view, about 50m uphill (left) of the first gate you saw. Walk over to this smaller gate.
(WP 119) (E 334368 N 540081 (NY 343400)).

5.6
300m

Bear slightly right through the gate, more or less maintaining height as you pass just right of the area of bracken and trees.

As you round this scrubby area, a stone wall will appear ahead of you with woodland behind it. Aim for the gate at the top (left) end of this wall.
(WP 120) (E 334672 N 540202 (NY 346402)).

5.7
300m

Heading for the gate at WP 120

There may be cause for a small celebration when this gate is reached –there's a CW waymark on it! And there are some more on a fallen-down waymark post stuck into a nearby pile of stones. You see, you're not lost after all. Go through the gate back into woodland, briefly on another recently relaid path. In 300m arrive at a way-marked gate with arrows directing you right downhill.
(WP 121) (E 334950 N 540309 (NY 349403)).

5.8
1km

Follow the arrows onto a narrower path with–in summer at least–tall vegetation on either side.

The path descends quite steeply: take care in wet weather as it gets very slippery. Also remember that you are still on a bridleway–you may find yourself having to give way to horse riders! As the path winds its way downhill through luxuriant vegetation, ignore a foot-path going off to the right at a waymark post and keep on descending until you reach the river bank at an attractive spot with some low cliffs on the opposite side of the river. Bear left with the path along the riverside, soon passing a sign warning of landslide and fallen rocks (even though mud appears to be a bigger hazard these days). A few minutes later leave the wood/river bank at a gate next to a miniature ladder stile and with a large flat rock, just crying out to be sat on, a few paces further on.
(WP 122) (E 335755 N 540681 (NY 357406)).

5.9 1.4km

Keep ahead staying just outside the edge of the wood and moving away from the riverside.

The path at first is just a line in the grass but, as it passes through gates, it becomes a cart track–overgrown at first but then much clearer. In a little less than a kilometre, pass a public footpath going off to the left to Warnell (*B&B at Lakelynn*). (The footpath is signed (to Low Parkhead, not Warnell) but access to it is difficult in summer because of rampant head-high weeds.)

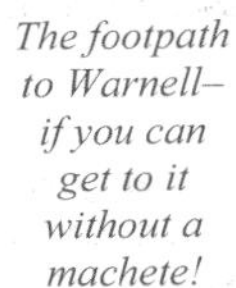

The footpath to Warnell–if you can get to it without a machete!

Keep ahead on the now obvious way to come to the road B5305 just left of Sebergham Bridge. Turn right to cross the bridge–take care of traffic!–and in 50m (just as the road bends right and starts to climb) turn left immediately after a house onto a path signposted for Sebergham Church. *(Strand Bank B&B is just before this down an unmarked lane on the right immediately after crossing Sebergham Bridge.) (Phone box 600m up road (SE) and pub 1km further.)* The CW path (overgrown at first) passes through a small wooden gate. **(WP 123)** (E 335801 N 541832 (NY 358418)).

5.10 600m

Now on grass, the path climbs half right up a bank to come out behind a large house and then onto a small surfaced road giving good views right to Carrock Fell and the fells around High Pike.

Pass a well-kept lawn with a flagpole and bench and in about 400m arrive at Sebergham Church. Just opposite the church gate is a track (Public Bridleway) going off to the left.
(WP 124) (E 336389 N 541865 (NY 363418)).

WP 124

St Mary's Church, Sebergham

5.11 1.3km

Take this track heading north. In 500m it passes right of a set of white gates.

Keep ahead with the grounds of Sebergham Hall (a farm) to your left, soon passing the Hall's front entrance. Stay on the main track which, in a further 350m, descends gently to a minor road. Turn left and cross Bell Bridge. On the right is a narrow gap stile with a sign-post to Rose Bridge.
(WP 125) (E 336580 N 543005 (NY 365430)).

Bell Bridge

For the next 4.5km, the route of the CW follows the bank of the River Caldew. In very wet conditions, it is possible that there might be problems with flooded fields making the way impassable. If the river has burst its banks and water is lying in the fields along the line of the path ahead, you might be better using footpaths and minor roads as far as Lime House School (paragraph 5.14): a suggested route is to go up the road east from Bell Bridge, soon going left onto a footpath to Greenfoot and on to turn left onto a minor road to Hudbeck. Then stay with small roads past Thethwaite, Breconhill, Haythwaite, and Raughton Head Church, to Rose Bridge (WP 126). If the fields are still flooded here keep straight on to climb away from the river and then turn right for Lime House School.

5.12
4.1km

Assuming there are no flooding problems, go through the gap stile taking care with the steep steps (a newish handrail makes it much less hazardous than it used to be).

For most of the next 4km to Rose Bridge just stay as near to the river as the path will allow. All along here stiles have recently been replaced by gates and there are some new footbridges. Notable features are: a tyre "hedge"; an attractive former mill on the left (see photo below), and, as a final reminder that you are no longer in the hill country of the Lake District, a place where you walk alongside barley and wheat fields.

The former mill at Lanehead

After about 1.3km (about 20 minutes), just after a section where the path goes along the top of an eroded steep bank, the route moves briefly away from the river to cross a deep-cut tributary stream at a footbridge. At first after this, there is no path, so head diagonally back to the riverbank. The field you are now in was laid out with horse jumps the last time the author was there (July 2011). Pass–but do not cross–a footbridge on the right (Bog Bridge) and then, almost immediately after that, ignore a footpath going left (to Welton). Pass a Citroën graveyard on the other side of the river and then, 250m further on, go through a gate into a wood. The walk through the wood is excellent but in 450m leave it at a gate, from where you get a first view of Rose Castle, until recently the home of the Bishops of Carlisle, but at the time of going to print, a building with an uncertain future. All will be revealed in the fullness of time no doubt.

There then follows more of the same–just stay by the river, following the obvious way–and come to a road at Rose Bridge. Cross the road but not the bridge and go ahead through a signposted kissing gate.
(WP 126) (E 337459 N 545920 (NY 374459)).

Rose Bridge

5.13
1.1km

Once through the gate there follows 700m of the same sort of walking–an obvious path alongside the river.

Then, where the river makes a big bend to the right, the path leaves it by maintaining its northerly direction towards the left-hand edge of the woodland ahead (Willowclose Wood). Cross a combined stile/bridge/duckboard affair and climb slightly to a gate 150m ahead. **(WP 127)** (E 337505 N 546923 (NY 375469)).

The combined stile/ bridge on the way up to the gate at WP 127. This photo was taken 2 or 3 years ago when the structure was new: it has weathered a bit since then

5.14
800m

Go through and keep just left of the first tree following a line in the grass for 200m to reach and go through a kissing gate onto a broad cart track at a three-way signpost.

Go left (SP Holm Hill and Dalston) and then head straight across the access road just in front of the impressive building of Lime House School. Go through a gate onto a bridleway across a sort of parkland with stately oak trees–all very pleasant but a very far cry from the wilds of Skiddaw Forest. Keep ahead in the same line and come to a gate just left of a modern white house. Bear left onto a cart track and soon come to a stone built house on your left. (*Left turn here for Hawksdale Lodge B&B.)* For the CW, keep ahead/half right (SP Dalston) on a small tarmac road that in about 250m ends just past the front entrance to Hawksdale Hall, where there is a gate in front of you.
(WP 128) (E 337508 N 547727 (NY 375477)).

5.15 1.5km	Go through the gate (SP for Dalston) onto a broad track that almost immediately swings left to climb gently to a gate beneath a tree.

Go straight on–(NB there could be plenty of cattle hereabouts)–with views to the right down to the valley of the Caldew. In 550m the track bends sharp left and comes to a gate onto a lane of houses. Walk down the lane and turn right onto the busy B5299. Follow the road down to the hamlet of Bridge End where there is a *pub and a phone box. There is also a bus service to Dalston and Carlisle.*

Bridge End

The main road sweeps round to the left here but the CW goes straight ahead along a smaller road (signposted for Durdar and the M6) to cross the Caldew at Hawksdale Bridge.
(WP 129) (E 337072 N 548756 (NY 370487)).

The short stretch of the CW from Hawksdale Bridge–all of 400 metres–has managed to provide walkers (and guide-book writers) with three alternatives: one is shown on the OS map so has a claim to be the official route; one is shown on the Harvey Map, and the third is not shown on the maps but is the way that just about everybody and nearly all the guide books appear to favour. It is this third option that we'll regard as the main one so that one will be described first.

5.16 400m

About 100m after the bridge, the road comes to a junction with a small road called Riverside which goes off to the left.

Bear right with the main road and, in a further 150m pass the former corn mill (now a house in the hamlet of Buckabank) and turn left just after it. Almost immediately arrive at the access road to Ellers Mill, currently run by a company called Cowens who, it seems, are "driven by excellence in customer care". (You, no doubt, will be driven by the urge to get to Carlisle.) Turn right onto the access road. **(WP 130)** (E 337133 N 549106 (NY 371491)).

*The **"Harvey Map" alternative** follows the main route over the bridge but, instead of staying with the main road, it goes left along the smaller road called Riverside. At the end of Riverside, turn right at the T-junction and, in 100m, arrive at the access road to Ellers Mill, where you turn left.*

*For the **third route** (the one shown on OS maps), turn right **immediately** after Hawksdale Bridge through a gate warning of farm livestock. There is also a signpost (SP Raughton Road). You are now on a footpath squeezed in between the river and a tall hedge/fence, through which you might catch a glimpse of some llamas. In about 150m walk alongside a fenced-off garden area (barking dogs) and arrive at a shady place with mud etc. and free-range poultry. Turn left through an unwaymarked white gate into a sort of lane with chicken runs. This soon gives onto an access road going away to the left. Cross this and climb a waymarked stile into a field. Walk across grass alongside a stream towards a row of white-painted houses. Reach the road where you join the main route. Turn right across the bridge, pass the former corn mill and turn left to come to the Ellers Mill access road.*

All three options are OK: the "off-road" one is theoretically the most attractive but walking past barking dogs–even ones behind fences–is not everyone's cup of tea. The occupier here seemed to be very friendly when the author stopped for a chat–it depends on how comfortable you are walking through unwaymarked property I suppose.

The two road routes are both provided with footways.

5.17 550m	Take the surprisingly sylvan access road–with a picturesque mill stream to your left–and then go through the mill complex, passing between the older mill on the left and some rather forlorn-looking newer buildings.

The access road to Ellers Mill

Pass beneath the tall chimney and leave the mill by passing a fairly posh house and then walking along another leafy tarmac lane that brings you out onto a small road.
(WP 131) (E 337095 N 549645 (NY 370496)).

There are suggestions that the next 4km (2½ miles) of the CW–as far as Cummersdale–should be re-routed via the east bank of the Caldew. If that should happen, these notes will be amended accordingly but, until then, they will continue to reflect the route as it now is i.e. via Dalston and the cycleway on the west side of the Caldew.

5.18 1.4km	Turn left and ignore the signed footpath on the right for Cummersdale. Cross the small bridge over the mill race and then the larger White Bridge over the Caldew.

Go along the lane to the main road at Dalston where a road sign tells you it is just 4¼ miles to Carlisle.

5.18 cont

Turn right into the main part of the village (convenience store, pub, café and other shops) and continue along the main road out of the village keeping left of the church.

Pass the post office and note the road sign that says you're further from Carlisle than you were a few minutes ago! *(A left turn here up Station Road will, believe it or not, take you to the railway station: trains for Carlisle, but they are not frequent. Check the timetables.)* Pass the primary school on the right and, immediately after it, turn right (SP Cummersdale). You're now on the tarmac cycle way which is almost dead level and so makes for easy, if somewhat tedious, walking. You also need to remain alert because it would seem that not all cyclists give adequate warning of their approach. There is a brief respite after 500m as an optional (unofficial) route goes off right at a WMP into woodland alongside the river.
(WP 132) (E 337433 N 550606 (NY 374506)).

5.19 3.3km

WP 132. If you're fed up with tarmac, bear right off the cycleway at this waymark post

Unless you really want to stay on the tarmac, bear right into the wood where the path bends this way and that but is easy to follow. After 450m it rejoins the tarmac cycle way. Follow this for the next 2.7km (including one dead straight stretch of 1.3km alongside the railway line). The way passes beneath some power lines and then, after what might seem like a long time, it goes under a very low railway bridge and 200m further, it comes out onto a road leading left to Cummersdale (*Phone box 700m up the hill in Cummersdale village)*. Don't take this but keep ahead and come to a footbridge (SP Blackwell). **(WP 133)** (E 339500 N 552930 (NY 395529)).

5.20
1.5km

Don't cross the bridge but keep straight ahead as if you were going to walk through the gates into the factory ahead of you.

Just as you reach the gates, though, head right onto a tarmac footpath that takes you between the mill and the river. This not very scenic stretch of about 350m ends when you arrive at a set of steps in front of you with a metal railing to the right. Don't climb the steps but leave the tarmac by staying right of the fence. Briefly, you're back on a woodland path but you soon leave it at a waymarked gate/stile that leads into a big field.

The footpath alongside the river between Cummersdale and Carlisle

Stay on the path nearest the river and keep going for almost a kilometre until the path starts to bend away from the river. Ignore the path that climbs up to a gate into an area of housing but stay nearer the river to reach a three-way signpost.
(WP 134) (E 339587 N 554338 (NY 395543)).

5.21
350m

Go right here onto a path between the river and a former mill building now converted into flats. Pass the weir–the Caldew's last great moment–from where there is a view back to the familiar, but now distant, fells around High Pike.

Looking back to High Pike from the Caldew weir

5.21 cont	Continue on past a building called Holme Head House to reach the end of Denton Street (left) and a substantial new footbridge on the right. (WP 135) (E 339824 N 554564 (NY 398545)).

From here, almost as far as Carlisle Castle, the CW follows the new footpath/cycleway, created partly as a by-product of the major flood relief works that have gone on here since the big flood of 2005 when the Caldew and the Eden both burst their banks and submerged much of Carlisle.

5.22 2.4km	From the end of Denton Street, keep ahead on the path that runs between the river and a children's playground to bring you to another new FB and the end of another street of terraced houses. (New CW waymarks here).

Keep ahead, this time onto McIlmoyle Way, a modern housing development. Pass the end of Metcalfe Street with its wooden arch and keep ahead again. Keep ahead past the end of Thomas Street (WM) and then, after a LH bend, make a quick right and left through a floodgate at the end of Lime Street. The walkway now follows the track of a dismantled railway line as it crosses the Caldew for one last time. There is a good view left to a tall mill chimney but the river has now lost its youthful exuberance and has become old and sluggish–very like the author.

Soon after this the cycleway/footpath turns sharp right and ends suddenly as it deposits you on an uninspiring thoroughfare that appears to be called Viaduct Estate Road. Turn left and walk up to a main road. Turn right and walk past the end of the spectacular Millennium Footbridge. (The CW no longer visits the Castle.)

The Millennium Footbridge leading to Carlisle Castle

If you want to visit the Castle, either cross the bridge or, if it's closed, keep on along Annetwell Street next to the dual carriageway until you can cross this by using the subway at the end of Castle Street by Tullie House museum.

From the footbridge, the official CW—with its new yellow WMs on lamp posts etc— keeps ahead alongside the dual carriageway and passes a Radio Cumbria office and the Tullie House museum to reach the end of Castle Street.

Turn right onto Castle Street where there are some new installations celebrating Carlisle's history and its place on Hadrian's wall. The appearance of the street itself has also been improved and the last few minutes of the walk are very pleasant as you pass the end of Paternoster Row and then the Cathedral. Continue a little further to reach the pedestrian area at the Market Cross just in front of the Old Town Hall, now the Tourist Information Centre.
(WP 136) (E 340074 N 555944 (NY 400559)).

The end of the CW at the Market Cross, Carlisle
The TIC is in the old Town Hall, the building in the photo

You've walked the Cumbria Way: well done! Crack open the fizz.

As a special bonus for you, the Tourist Information Centre has a "log-book" of the walk and walkers who have completed the Cumbria Way are encouraged to add details of their journey and comments about the route. If you have anything to say about the CW –especially about matters such as waymarking, the state of the footpaths (including gates and stiles etc.) and the facilities on the route– please go in and make your views known: it all helps to keep the route alive and kicking!

Carlisle makes a fitting end to a long-distance walk. Its castle and cathedral are worth a visit, and the short stroll along the West Walls is great, especially on a clear day when you may well catch a distant glimpse of the Lake District fells.

There is plenty of accommodation in Carlisle, a mainline railway station with direct trains to most parts of the UK (including London and Glasgow), and, of course, loads of shops and services.

CARLISLE

(www.openstreetmap.org)
(The CW/cycleway follows the line of blue dots by the river.)

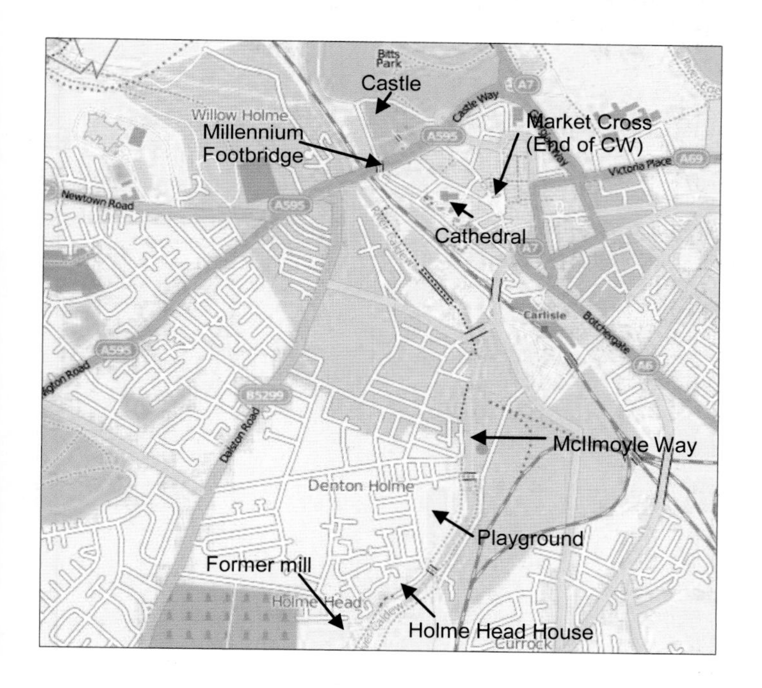

Cumbria Way–Contact Details Accommodation

Name and Address	Phone	Email	Arrival Date

Baggage Transfer Providers

Name and Address	Phone	Email

Notes

Notes

Notes

Notes

Notes

Notes

Notes

Notes